...Continued

It does not seem that over five years have passed since we introduced the first edition of LEELANAU COUNTRY INN COOKERY-FOOD AND WINE FROM THE LAND OF DELIGHT, but it has.

Linda and I could not have been more pleased with the many fine comments and notes received from that project. After numerous requests we decided to do it again!

We bring back the quality you found in the first edition with nearly 100 new recipes and 55 new illustrations and update the history a bit with the changes that have taken place over the past five years. This edition adds an extra helping hand by showing you where you can purchase many of the key ingredients we use at the Inn.

We hope you will enjoy reading about the Inn, its staff, its purveyors and, of course, some more of our favorite recipes.

-Linda and John Sisson

VOLUME 2

LEELANAU COUNTRY INN COOKERY... CONTINUED

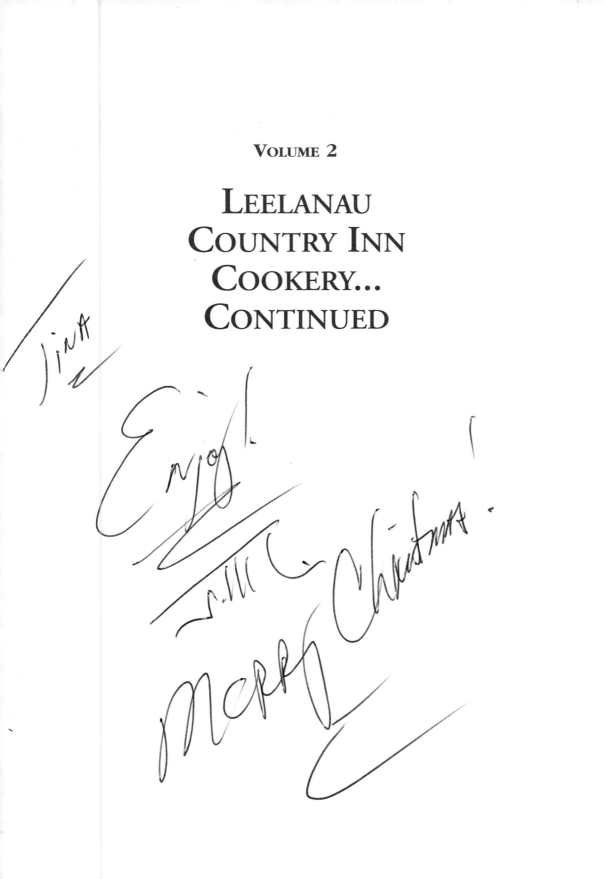

Jim
Enjoy!
with
Merry Christmas.

VOLUME 2

LEELANAU COUNTRY INN COOKERY... CONTINUED

FOOD AND WINE FROM THE LAND OF DELIGHT

BY LINDA & JOHN SISSON

ILLUSTRATED BY PEGGY CORE
WITH MATERIAL ON WINE BY LARRY MAWBY

THE BUCCA PRESS
Maple City, Michigan

The Bucca Press
149 East Harbor Hwy.
Maple City, MI 49664

Front & Back Cover Photograph by Michael Cole,
Traverse City, Michigan

Interior Illustrations by Peggy Core, Suttons Bay, Michigan

Cover Design by Jim DeWildt, Traverse City, Michigan
Interior Design by Peggy Core & Jim DeWildt

Proofreading by Virginia & Frank Sisson

First Edition

Publisher's Cataloging-in-Publication Data
Sisson, Linda, 1952-
Leelanau Country Inn Cookery ...Continued: food and wine from the land of
delight / by Linda & John Sisson; illustrated by Peggy Core; with material on
wines by Larry Mawby. –Maple city, Mich.: Bucca Press, 2000
p.   cm.
ISBN-0-9676535-0-9
LCCN-99-68157

1. Leelanau Country Inn–History. 2. Cookery, American. 3. Wine lists. 4.
Menus. I. Sisson, John, 1953 - II. Title.
TX715 .S627   2000
641.5973–dc21   CIP

Project Coordination by Jenkins Group, Inc.

02 01 00 99 ▲ 5 4 3 2 1

Printed in the United States of America

Grace...
Come Lord Jesus Be Our Guest
And Let These Gifts to Us Be Blessed.

-Amen

"MUCH TOO EARLY"

John Andrew Petersen, Linda's father, went home to be with the
Lord May 25, 1967, much too early. Linda was only thirteen at
the time; this strong loving man shaped her life. He has been and
continues to be missed! Linda's mother, Lucille Petersen Bach,
synonymous with GREAT FOOD, has been a mainstay in the
Leland area her entire life. Lucille's culinary talents have been a
legend in her own time and an inspiration to us both.
Lucille went home to be with the Lord November 7, 1999.

Mother and Dad, we dedicate this to you!

TABLE OF CONTENTS

GREAT BEGINNINGS   57

SOUPS, SALADS & SIDE DISHES   73

PASTA AT THE INN   83

LAKE & OCEAN FISH AND OTHER OCEAN FAVORITES   97

POULTRY & MEAT   131

THANKSGIVING ACCOMPANIMENTS   147

PERFECT ENDINGS   165

RECIPES REVISITED   191

AN EDITOR'S INTRODUCTION

"Go thy way. Eat thy bread with joy, and drink
thy wine with merry heart; for God now
accepteth thy works."

-Ecclesiastes

Back in October of 1993, Linda and I met with Larry Mawby and Peggy Core to explore the idea of a cookbook that encompassed wine and cookery fundamentals, recipes of our most requested favorites and in general "something more than a cookbook". Well, in May of 1994, at the occasion of our tenth anniversary, we produced just that. Our first edition of LEELANAU COUNTRY INN COOKERY-FOOD AND WINE FROM THE LAND OF DELIGHT went over well beyond our expectations. The comments and reviews have been overwhelming, and the requests for even more recipes became too numerous to ignore. So here we go again! The following will give you a good idea of what to expect in our second book, LEELANAU COUNTRY INN COOKERY ...CONTINUED!-FOOD AND WINE FROM THE LAND OF DELIGHT.

In the book's first chapter, we welcome you back to the Inn, reintroducing you to our "kids" and catching up on what has taken place over the past five years in that area. We let you meet a few of the many staff members that make your visit to the Inn pleasant and memorable and tell you about our relationship with our purveyors and the importance they play in our success as they consistently supply the Inn with quality food and other necessary supplies. Finally, we round out the introductions with a bit of our personal history at the Inn. Reading this chapter will leave you with no doubt that the people of the Inn continue to be its most important asset.

In the chapter "The Wine List," Larry Mawby has contributed some information on another important part of the Leelanau Country Inn experience, the wines produced by Leelanau Peninsula's first four local vintners. Over the first fifteen years, the Inn has featured the products of our area's wineries to the virtual exclusion of all other wines. In the spring of 1999 we expanded our wine list to include some foreign wines and California favorites. Because Mawby, Boskydel, Good Harbor and Leelanau Ltd. pioneered winemaking on the Peninsula, we have decided to highlight only their wines on our local list. In addition to a bit of information about each winery's place in the local scene and their wines, the chapter includes a categorization of some wines and a few principles useful in matching foods and wines. These principles are demonstrated later in the book, as each entrée recipe has suggestions for the appropriate wines for service with that entrée. This chapter also has a profile on a great friend to the Inn, Larry Mawby.

Before the recipes commence, we've included a short chapter entitled "Cookery Fundamentals." *It is important that even the experienced cook reads this before proceeding to the recipes themselves,* as this chapter outlines the basic assumptions we've made about ingredients, equipment and techniques used in the kitchen. The notation system used is explained-of particular import is the Shamrock (☘), signifying that the recipe so marked requires extended preparation time. All the recipes in this book have been test prepared at the scale given here, and, to the extent possible, the use of specialized kitchen equipment has been avoided. Also, attention has been given to the problem of finding ingredients for home use. In a very few cases, recipes have been altered and test cooked with new, easier to find ingredients.

In preparing to cook, using the recipes in this book, it is vital that good kitchen technique be used. Be aware of the time required to prepare the dish. Read the recipe through, noting where ingredients themselves are the product of recipes in this book, and prepare those ingredients as required. Assemble all equipment and ingredients before beginning to assemble the dish—trimming, cleaning, slicing, dicing, etc. as required. Only when everything is laid out and ready for use should the actual assembly of the dish begin. You'll find that, when appropriate, the recipes contain hints (Δ) about cooking techniques used by the professional chef, and that most of them also include suggested substitutions for ingredients, or variations (◊) on preparation and service instructions.

As to the nine chapters of recipes themselves, note that the first chapter "Breadings, Stuffings, Sauces & Dressings" is a compendium of recipes, several of which are components that are used in other recipes. You will be referring often to this chapter as you prepare recipes found in later chapters.

"Great Beginnings" offers a selection of appetizers, some of which might be scaled up and used as entrées, all of which are tasteful starters for a memorable meal. Specific wine selections are not made with the appetizers, in part because we feel a simple rule applies: always enjoy sparkling wines with appetizers at the beginning of a meal, frequently continue with a sparkling wine during the meal, and generally conclude the meal by sipping a bit of sparkling wine with dessert.

"Soups, Salads & Side Dishes" contains a group of recipes that fill out the menu, providing a complement to the showcase entrée, and a bridge between the appetizer and main course. When served with selections from "Great Beginnings," those dishes make a nice luncheon meal.

Then it's on to the three entrée chapters: "Pasta at the Inn," "Lake & Ocean Fish and Other Ocean Favorites" and "Poultry & Meat." As you look over entrée recipes, note that in most cases they have been scaled to serve 4 to 6 people. Generally, this is a scale up from the Inn's general practice of individual entrée preparation. Also, several possible substitutes are given for the main ingredient, making each recipe a mini-cookbook in itself. Note also that each entrée recipe includes a suggested dinner menu composed of other recipes in the book - useful meal planning advice. In addition, in these three chapters, wine service suggestions are given for each entrée.

"Thanksgiving Accompaniments" contains recipes used yearly at the Inn's Thanksgiving Buffet.

The final chapter, "Recipes Revisited," is a collection of recipes from our first edition of LEELANAU COUNTRY INN COOKERY-FOOD AND WINE FROM THE LAND OF DELIGHT. They are included because they are either needed as an ingredient in this edition or they are such standouts that those not having the first cookbook should not be deprived.

To help you find your way through the book, in addition to the Table of Contents where all the recipes are listed, an Index is provided that lists every occurrence of each recipe. Useful, for example, if you would really like to try a particular recipe and want to find every suggested menu that calls for that dish, or to see if a particular recipe is used as a component of another recipe. Also indexed are major ingredients, whether its called for in the recipe's ingredient list or listed as a variation. This should be useful if, for example, you've gotten some fresh Whitefish, and want to find every recipe that might be prepared using Whitefish.

Throughout the book, the pen and ink drawings by Peggy Core serve to beautify the page, clarify complex instructions, and illustrate ingredients, tools and the "kids". Her artwork reminds us that cookery, a domestic art, when done well, nourishes the spirit as well as the body, elevating cookery to a higher art. Peggy's drawings work to make this book 'more than a cookbook.'

"Knowledge is like a garden:
if it is not cultivated,
it cannot be harvested."
-Folk lore from Guinea

WELCOME BACK
TO THE
COUNTRY INN

"Of all the needs a book has the chief need
is that it be readable."

-Anthony Trollpe

For those of you that have been to the Inn or at least know a little about us, you know that our "kids" all have four legs and wagging tails. Our first child, Sambucca Anne, a Bearded Collie, came to our family two days after we were married in September of 1981. Sambucca died after fifteen-and-a-half years of unwavering, unconditional love. She set a standard in our home that her predecessors try to live up to. Although each and every one has her strong points, no one comes close to 'Bucca'. She remains our true love!

In January 1992, Ditto Lee, a Bichon Frise, joined the family; we lost her to a rare ailment at the young age of six. She left her mark on the family as well. She too is missed.

Back in August of 1990 came our now eldest child, Whitney Elizabeth. Another Bearded Collie, Whitney has grown through the years in age and size only. She still acts like a child, BARKS like a 'dog' (we don't, as a rule, use the "d" word) and generally does what she wants when she wants. Seniority has its place and she knows it. Sambucca she is not.

Moira Lyn joined the family in the fall of 1994. A beautiful black-and-white trim Beardie with long, flowing hair, majestic in appearance and attitude, she's our 'queen' and she makes sure we don't forget it. Then in the fall of 1997 came Bailey! A true bouncin' Beardie, she has energy that, if we could bottle it, would make us very wealthy people. Bailey has no intention of growing up and she keeps us on our toes every minute. She worms her way into your heart like no one since Sambucca!

In September of 1992, Linda and I had the extreme pleasure of meeting Jean and Irwin Richland, the proud owners of Melita Road Bearded Collies. Jean and Irwin were in Detroit for the national Bearded Collie Specialty Show and had three of their Beardies with them. After the show they traveled north for a little rest and relaxation before venturing back to California. While in a campground in Traverse City they came upon The Leelanau Country Inn's ad in the Record Eagle, our local newspaper; it showed an ink drawing of Sambucca and they "had" to meet the local Beardie owners. They came out to the Inn and we became fast friends. It's hard not to like a Beardie owner! Moira Lyn and Bailey Jean came from Melita Road Bearded Collies and Molly Marie is due February 2000. Jean and Irwin have been such an important part of the Sisson family that we would like to take this time to introduce them to you.

There isn't a time that Jean Richland, owner of Melita Road Bearded Collies, doesn't remember either running after a dog or holding and hugging one. From WWII, when, at the age of four, she tried to bring her elegant Irish Setter, Jill, into the house because of black-out sirens, through today, when she exhibits and judges Herding Breeds as a licensed A.K.C. Judge, Jean has focused her life around dogs... just ask her six children and her husband! Her first glimpse of a Beardie was at the Crufts Dog Show in London, England, back in the mid 1960s. It was at that point that she fell in love with the shaggy bouncin' Scottish Sheep Dog, and for the last 35 years she has continued that love affair by exhibiting, breeding and judging.

Over the years, Melita Road Bearded Collies has proudly produced over sixty champions and Jean has placed puppies all over the United States and in many foreign countries. Melita North Star (Moira Lyn), Melita Nina (Bailey Jean) and fast approaching Melita My Golly Its (Molly Marie) are three lucky Beardie girls to have had such adoring "parents". Melita Road Bearded Collies is located in sunny Riverside, California at the home of Jean and Irwin Richland.

9

Look for the "Kids' Choice" entries when dining in the recipe section!

As in the first edition, we have profiled some of the staff members that make the Inn the special place that it is. The tradition goes on. First an update: Our niece, Stephanie Tietje, who was portrayed as a soon-to-be attorney, is now one in the flesh! She is a proud graduate of Wake Forest and now works in the offices of the Chief Justice of the Michigan Supreme Court, Betty Weaver.

Chris (our nephew) Tietje, known at the Inn as 'T', is now a fifteen-year veteran and has risen to the role of Kitchen Manager. Chris started his career at the Inn at age eight in the dish room. His hard work and dedication to excellence promoted him through the ranks over the years and he is now responsible for the total kitchen operation. He has done an outstanding job. Few individuals over the 30-plus years I have been in business have impressed me more. He has earned his position by his talents and not by nepotism; he is a backbone to our success.

Not to miss out on the Millennium craze, we too got into the act by presenting two "Employee of the Millennium" awards at our April 1999 staff meeting. The first went to Sue Murphy. Sue has been a member of our team since the fall of 1986. Our head server and leader of the troops, Sue has been an anchor to our success. A tribute to her talents is the fact that she has countless guests at the Inn request her service.

The other "Employee of the Millennium" award went to Patty Leach. An anchor in the kitchen operation, Patty has been with us since the fall of 1987. It is very rare in this industry to have members of your staff stay in one place for so long. A big reason for our success is that we have been blessed with many employees who have given years and years of service at the Inn. We thank them, each and every one!

So what is the secret to the Inn's recipes? Is it the preparation, the cooking medium, the "titch" of this or that, or the special ingredients? We can assure you that we want to share our favorite recipes with all the steps involved. One thing that may appear to be mysterious is "Where does the Inn buy their ingredients from?" We will tell you where and, more importantly, from whom and why.

Another key to our longevity has been our relationship with two very important purveyors. Steve Connolly Seafood out of Boston has been our main source of fresh seafood since the early 70s. They remain our one and only purveyor of Fresh Ocean Fish.

Our second essential purveyor is Gordon Food Service. An adendum to this edition of the cookbook is a complete listing of Gordon Food Service (GFS) Marketplace stores throughout the Midwest. These stores are designed with the general public in mind, allowing everyone to purchase the same products we purchase so that you can obtain the same high quality results in your recipes. We took the time to introduce the GFS family in our first edition. However, their part in our success was not duly recognized then; therefore, we would now like to tell you the story of this remarkable business and the family behind it.

In May of 1999, at a special celebration of the fifteenth anniversary of the Leelanau Country Inn, we celebrated our longstanding relationship with Gordon Food Service by presenting them with our "Purveyor of the Millennium" award. We enjoyed a very special night with the Chairman of Gordon Food Service, Mr. Paul Gordon, and his wife, Dottie; the Vice Chairman, Mr. John Gordon, and his wife, Nancy; the President, Mr. Dan Gordon, and his wife, Magee; Operations Manager, Mr. Jim Gordon, and his wife, Bonnie, along with many other executives and key GFS associates.

To give you a quick, meaningful overview of Gordon Food Service, I would like to reprint the GFS "Philosophy Statement" that was in our first edition. This gives you a good idea why we choose to deal exclusively with them.

"Our Philosophy is simple:

ON CHANGE: We believe that change is a way of life; we should welcome it, we should look forward to it; we should create and force change, we should not wait to react to change by others.

ON GROWTH: We believe in controlled permanent growth for both the company and the individual. We will only grow as a company if we grow individually. Further, we believe that each person's contribution is meaningful and that each person helping us grow is entitled to share in such growth through sharing in company profits and meaningful individual incentive based on individual performance.

ON BUSINESS CONDUCT: We believe in complete integrity with each other, our customers, our suppliers and our community. Most important is the complete openness of information, and the ability for everyone to accept constructive ideas from each other.

ON THE RACE OF LIFE: We believe to be complete people we must succeed and not fail; we must not drift aimlessly and without purpose; that the race will indeed be won by the swift. Accordingly, each of us, and therefore our company, must be among the swift.

FINALLY: We believe in God, who sent his son, Jesus Christ, to earth to show us himself, and for us to be complete people, we must accept him by faith."

We suppose all companies have a stated philosophy, whether in print or not. A key difference with Gordon Food Service is that they practice their philosophy as a way of life. When you can deal with a company like this, why look elsewhere? We don't.

The Leelanau Country Inn purchases 100% of our produce, meats, dairy and general food products from Gordon Food Service in Grand Rapids, Michigan. Gordon Food Service is the largest independent food service distributor in America and is over 100 years old. They stock over 13,000 items that have been sourced from around the globe; they include GFS brand products, GFS exclusive brand products and national brand products. Their commitment to being first in the market with innovative products and services has made them the leader in the food service industry. Gordon Food Service is the only food distributor in the world with an on-site USDA-accredited lab, which tests foods using official and industry approved methods. With food safety a growing concern among consumers and food operators alike, Gordon Food Service takes the necessary precautions to help insure the quality and safety of their products.

In looking for a supplier for the Inn, Gordon Food Service, a fourth generation family business, appealed to us because they have many of the same philosophies about taking care of their customers as we have about taking care of our guests. We both believe in our staff and the commitment of true professionally trained employees. We want to offer expert knowledge, authenticity and excellence in our guests' dining experience. We share the belief in making a positive impression on our guests with the food we serve and the continual introduction of new and exciting menu selections. Last and most important, we both believe in keeping our promises to you, our valued guest.

Where do you purchase the ingredients for the Inn's special recipes . . . That's right, GFS Marketplace stores.

There are over 70 retail locations in a four-state area. Hopefully, one of these stores is not far from your local neighborhood. The GFS Marektplace stores are the places where professionals shop for products and personal food service needs.

Their goal for satisfying their customers (our guests) is the same as ours. At GFS Marketplace, the largest corporate accounts and the smallest consumer requests receive the same personal attention. They stock over 2,500 products, offer product information, special orders within 48 hours, computerized menu planning and low wholesale prices without any membership fees. To find the location nearest you, visit their website at www.gfs.com. A complete list is also in the Index.

We invite you to share the positive experience we've enjoyed with Gordon Food Service over the years in preparing these recipes. We recommend a phone call first to inquire if your local Marketplace store stocks the items listed in the recipe. If the store does not stock the item on a regular basis, they are able to get any of the 13,000 items within 48 hours and have it available for you to pick up.

The Leland Mercantile, Leland Michigan, owned and operated by Joe & Joni Burda is another great source for not only the products needed to prepare the recipes in this book but also they are the only source for some of our prepared items such as our Herbal Bread and Linguini Pasta. Joe and Joni have been the owners of the Mercantile since 1983. They bought their dream about six months before Linda and I secured the Inn. Like Linda and me, the Burdas have dedicated themselves to creating more than a grocery store. You will find specialty items in this Leland business that you will not find in most stores away from the city. Their commitment to the finest meats, produce and local specialty items makes the Merc the place to shop when in the Leland area.

Linda and I find ourselves with a combined sixty years plus experience in the restaurant business. We are now in our sixteenth year at the Inn. Linda, a native of Leland, and I, a June of 1980 transplant from the city, were married in September of 1981. In the Spring of 1984, we acquired the Inn and have been its innkeepers ever since. Now with our nephew, Chris Tietje, a 15-year veteran of the Inn at the helm in the kitchen, we have a true "family" operation.

The main house of the Inn was built in 1890, with the balance of the house built in 1895. Originally the home of Fred and Ruth Atkinson, it was christened the Traverse Lake Resort, and has housed travelers, under various ownership, since then.

We opened our doors on the 20th of May and over the past 15 years have welcomed over 625,000 guests. During that time, the Inn has increased its seating from 100 to 150 by adding a side porch area. We have tripled the size of the kitchen operation and, in doing so, created what is thought to be the only temperature controlled preparation room in the area; every refrigerated product that is served is prepped under refrigeration. Food does not hit the heat of the kitchen until it is time to be cooked.

All staff members are thoroughly trained for the positions they hold. The wait staff is provided with a documented training manual that reviews all areas related to service and to the product. Ongoing training is given to be sure nothing has been forgotten or overlooked. It is our strong belief that the only way to totally serve our guests is to insure that the staff has all the necessary tools and product knowledge.

The Leelanau Country Inn menu, which is Northern Michigan's most extensive, is printed daily. All of its items are prepared by recipe to insure consistency from visit to visit. All products are prepped daily and cooked to order the night of service. While the Inn specializes in seafood and fresh fish from the ocean (provided by Steve Connolly Seafood of Boston) and Michigan lakes

(provided by Carlson's Fish Market of Traverse City), there is also a wide variety of meats and fresh homemade pasta with a generous array of exciting sauces.
Our signature soup, Swiss Onion, has been featured in Gourmet and our wine list is comprised of the finest wines of Leelanau Country, California and overseas.

Diners can catch a glimpse of Little Traverse Lake across the road, marvel at the magnificent birch trees gracing the Inn's front yard, and take a stroll through the beautiful gardens created by Linda and added to and nurtured by her over the years.

It has been a rewarding 15 plus years for both of us, thanks to the many people who have worked with us in making the Leelanau Country Inn a favorite Northern Michigan dining spot, and to the many guests who keep coming back and keep spreading the word. A special thank you to Mr. John Visser for continuing to have faith in the Inn.

To all of you we express our sincere appreciation.

-Linda Sisson

-John Sisson

THE WINE LIST

"I love everything that's old; old friends, old times, old manners, old books, old wines."

-Goldsmith

The wine list at the Leelanau Country Inn is mainly comprised of the products of Leelanau Peninsula's wineries. This is very much a European country inn style list, recognizing local products as an integral part of one's daily life, with out-of-the-area wines and other foods served only as an added treat.

Locally produced wines offer us something special, in the same way that we enjoy tomatoes fresh from our backyard garden, or sweet corn picked and boiled immediately, or a juicy peach eaten under the tree on which it grew. Not only do these special foods taste good, but through them our immediate connection with the earth renews us. Those of us fortunate enough to live close to the land enjoy this connection while the urban and suburban dweller is drawn to places like Leelanau County by the desire for it. Fortunately, at places like the Country Inn, anyone has the opportunity to sit down and reestablish those natural connections in the company of family and friends.

But wine, unlike the fresh tomato, sweet corn, or peach, can travel through time as well as space. With wine, one can experience on a cold, bitter January day in 2000, the warmth, the joy, the life of the summer of 1995. Open a bottle of 1995 vintage, pour a glass and smell the bouquet time has brought to the aromas of the grapes harvested years before, sip and savor the flavor of that season past, let it join in memory with the meal today. It is this ability to transcend time and place that has made wine such an intriguing part of our lives.

Sadly, all too often we are kept from this pleasurable experience by our fear of doing something wrong. We have exalted wine to a special place, surrounding it with mystery and barely understood ritual, and fear to intrude. This is unfortunate. Though wine may be a mystery, its enjoyment, and its place at the table need not be. One surely does not need to know exactly how an airplane works, nor how to pilot it, in order to let an airline take you away to that longed-for idyllic vacation spot. Neither do you need to know much about wine to let it grace your table.

There are no rules about selecting and serving wine. If you are a person that must have rules, then there is only one rule - serve the wine you like with the food you like. If guidance is desired (without the strictures of rule-making), we can offer a few hints that will, we hope, increase your enjoyment of the meal and the wine. When matching wines with foods, consider the dominant flavor or aroma of the food, how intense it is; consider the flavors and aroma of the possible wine companions. If you are making a match that's intended to highlight the food, select a wine with complementary, though less intense, flavors and aromas. This wine will act like the second and third players in the orchestra section, deepening and filling in the sound of the first player, in this case the food. If you wish to highlight the wine, select an intensely flavored wine with flavors complementary to a lighter food, or, more difficult, a wine of intensity that contrasts with an intense food.

We have, in our own mind, divided the wines of Leelanau Peninsula into a few categories that make it easier to identify complementary and contrasting food and wine pairings. These categories are very simple, so simple, in fact, that many wines donít really fit into categories.

All sparkling wines are in a category of their own (from the Leelanau Peninsula, sparkling wines are almost always dry or very nearly so, with flavors and aromas hearkening to the classic French Champagne). Honesty compels me to confess that I am one of the only producers of sparkling wines from the Leelanau Peninsula;

however, my description of them is without prejudice. When we encounter red wines, we've divided them into three categories - dry light red, dry medium red and semi-dry red. There really aren't any heavy red wines produced in Leelanau (this is one place the Country Inn balances the wine list with wines from elsewhere).

In the case of white wines from Leelanau Peninsula, the selection is much greater, and the range is larger. We've divided white wines into several categories - dry light white, dry medium white, dry heavy white, semi-dry light white, semi-dry medium white and semi-dry heavy white. Since the categorization system is intended for offering suggestions with dinner entrees, we have not included any sweet wines. This is my personal preference, but remember the rule - there are no rules - so if you wish, by all means enjoy a sweet wine, of any color and weight, with your meal.

Now, what are dry or semi-dry wines? By dry wines, we mean those which have no perceptible sugary flavor. This does not mean that a dry wine might not have fruit flavors so intense that they bring to mind the memory of sweet, ripe fruit; but rather that they do not have a sugary character. Semi-dry wines, on the other hand, have some of this sugary character, though it is not dominant as would be the case with sweet wines. Semi-dry wines live in both the dry and sweet worlds, partaking a bit of both characters. My personal preference amongst semi-dry wines, with most foods, is a wine that smells of sweet fruits, tastes initially of ripe fresh fruit, and then, in the back of the mouth, displays a pleasant crispness that refreshes the palate.

We have also given three weights of wines: light, medium and heavy. This has nothing to do with any scale measure, but rather the sum of several parts of the perception of the wine. For me, the weight of the wine is what others call 'body' plus other factors like tannin, fruit intensity, and even color. Light wines have minimal tannins (tannins produce the sensation of astringency, like the 'bite' of tea); generally lower levels of alcohol (alcohol contributes to the feel of the wine in the mouth, more alcohol making the wine feel 'fuller, rounder' and also 'hotter'); and generally the fruit flavors play a greater part in the totality of the wine's flavor, though they will themselves be lesser in intensity in a light wine than in a heavy wine. Heavy wines are the other end of the taste spectrum, with much more tannic astringency, generally a greater weight of alcohol, and with other flavors (often those contributed by oak barrel aging) that underlie or surround the fruit flavors inherent in the wine, buoying and making more massive the entire flavor structure. Obviously, medium weight wines are the most easily paired with entrees, as they can play a second string to a spicy dish, or be the first string when playing with a delicately flavored entree.

Using the descriptions above, and this simple categorization system, should help you in communicating your desires when purchasing wine, either in a store or at a restaurant. Any trained wine salesperson can point out several candidates if asked, for example, for a dry, medium-weight white wine. Later in this book, in the entree recipes, John and Linda offer a specific wine suggestion identified by these categories. This should help you find substitute wines if you are unable to find a specific suggested wine (unfortunately, Leelanau Peninsula wines are, like fresh fish, not universally available, so substitutes are sometimes necessary). John has included a suggested wine for each entree, with a specific example of a Leelanau Peninsula wine in each case.

And what of the producers of the wines on the list at the Country Inn? By the end of 1999 there will be nine wineries on the Leelanau Peninsula. As mentioned before, we have chosen to present the four pioneers in

the county. This Land of Delight is blessed with pic-
turesque rolling hills, clear lakes and streams, clean air,
and a charming diversity of seasons. Agriculture has been
an important part of the life of the Peninsula since mod-
ern settlement in the 1800s. Most recently, starting in the
early 1970s, wine grape growing and wine making has
come to Leelanau. More vines are being planted each
year, and production of the area's dry red and white, semi-
dry white and sparkling wines continues to increase.

Boskydel Vineyard, located south of the village of Lake
Leelanau on a hillside overlooking the lake, is the area's
oldest winery. Bernie Rink pioneered wine grape growing
in this area, first planting a small backyard vineyard in
1963. Further plantings followed, and a winery was
established in 1976. Today Boskydel produces a range of
dry and semi-dry red, white and rosé table wines from
several direct producer varieties grown in those vineyards.
Boskydel is perhaps best known for dry and semi-dry
reds and rosés from the deChaunac grape variety and dry
and semi-dry whites from the Vignoles and Seyval
grapes. Soleil Blanc is a unique dry white produced from
a direct producer variety grown nowhere else.

Good Harbor Vineyards, located south of Leland with
the winery overlooking Good Harbor Bay and with
additional vineyards near Sugar Loaf Mountain, is the
largest grower on the Peninsula. Bruce Simpson's Good
Harbor vineyard, first planted in 1978, today produces a
range of dry and semi-dry red, white and rosé table
wines from several vinifera and direct producer varieties,
as well as a particularly pleasant cherry wine. The winery
is best known for a series of excellent semi-dry white
wines, such as Trillium, Northern Lights and Fishtown
White; dry whites from Vignoles, Chardonnay and Pinot
Gris, and semi-dry white Riesling.

Leelanau Wine Cellars, the second oldest winery on the
Peninsula, is the largest producer. The winery is located
at Omena, with vineyards there and also southwest of

Suttons Bay. Again, the winery produces a range of
wines, primarily from direct producer varieties, with
increasing amounts of vinifera, that has included at times
dessert wines like ports or ice wines in addition to red,
white and rosé table wines, dry semi-dry and sweet.
The mainstays of the winery are the semi-dry 'seasonal
blends', Winter White, Spring Splendor and Summer
Sunset; the dry red and white Vis · Vis; and dry whites
from Vignoles and Chardonnay. The fruit wines of
Leelanau Wine Cellars are also notable.

L. Mawby Vineyards is located in the hills south of
Suttons Bay, with vineyards adjacent to the winery.
Our vineyards were established in 1973, and additional
plantings have been made subsequently, today yielding
a range of sparkling wines as well as dry and semi-dry
white table wines, from both disease resistant and
verifera varieties. We are perhaps best known as a
producer of methode champenoise sparkling wines,
particularly our estate-grown vineyard designated cuvees
Cremant and Talisman, and our vintage dated tete de
cuvee, Mille; as well as our Blanc de Blanc, from
Chardonnay grapes grown by other growers on the
Leelanau Peninsula. We were honored to have been
named recently by The Wine Enthusiast as a Great
Sparkling Wine Producer. And we are pleased to have
produced for many years the Leelanau Country Inn
private label wines—Sambucca, Whitney, Moira, Ditto
and Bailey. We also produce dry white wines from estate-
grown Vignoles and Pinot Gris, and a semi-dry white
wine called Sandpiper, as well as wines like Chardonnay
and Riesling with grapes purchased from other growers.

In the past decade the growing of wine grapes and the
making of wines has become an established feature of
the Leelanau Peninsula. At the time that the present
Leelanau Country Inn came under the ownership of
Linda and John Sisson, there were only four growers
and associated wineries. Today, the number of growers
is nearly two dozen, and there are more than nine

wineries producing Leelanau Peninsula wines. At the Leelanau Country Inn, the wine list has grown to include more wines from around the world, yet it has retained a local focus on the original four wineries, continuing to fulfill the Inn's promise of fine food and wine from the Land of Delight.

-Larry Mawby

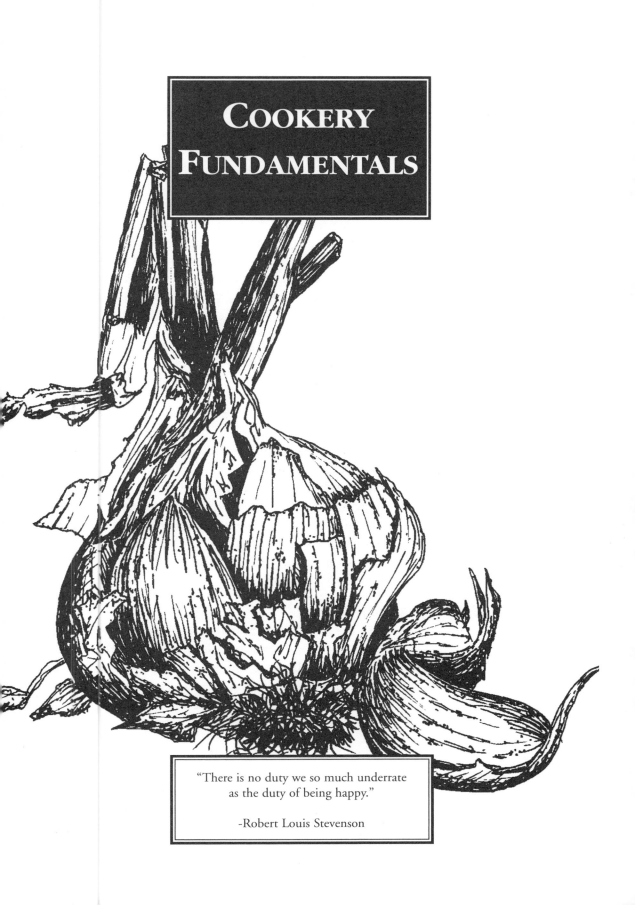

COOKERY
FUNDAMENTALS

"There is no duty we so much underrate
as the duty of being happy."

-Robert Louis Stevenson

There are many fundamental principles that underlie the instructions given in any cookbook. We've attempted in this section to detail the important assumptions we've made in writing this cookbook. These include details about preparation techniques, ingredient selection, cookery tools and serving.

As you read through the recipes, you will note that three symbols are used to direct your attention to additional information.

♣ The Shamrock, found next to the recipe name in the Table of Contents and on the page with the recipe, means that some additional preparation time is required. This additional time may range from a few hours, in the case of dishes that must be chilled before serving, to a day or more, in the case of marinated dishes or recipes that use sauces best made in advance in order that the flavors may meld. In any case, the preparation instructions for the recipe will give you an idea of how much extra time is required.

Δ The Pyramid, found alongside an ingredient listing or in the preparation instructions, directs your attention to a Hint about the recipe, found after the preparation instructions. Hints are meant to help you with preparation techniques, or explain why a particular preparation method is used. If several Hints are included with a recipe, they are numbered, for example, Δ2.

◊ The Diamond, seen generally alongside an ingredient, directs you to a Variation for the recipe, found after the Hints that follow the preparation instructions. Variations generally refer to substitute ingredients that may be used, though in some cases they may include additional ingredients or preparation steps. The Variations sometimes include changes in basic ingredients that, if used, remake the recipe to yield a new dish. If several Variations are included with a recipe, they are numbered, for example, ◊3.

THE SETS The first rule of cookery is to take time to read the recipe before starting to make the dish, then assemble all required equipment and ingredients, chopping, dicing, slicing, etc., as required. This assemblage of equipment and ingredients is called the set. Only after these preparations are made is the set ready and the assembly of the dish to commence. Following this fundamental rule is of particular importance in these recipes, as many include as part of their ingredients the product of another recipe elsewhere in the book. Planning is essential to the preparation of virtually every recipe in this book.

INGREDIENTS We cannot emphasize too strongly the importance in cookery of quality ingredients. The Inn brings in all of its ingredients through Gordon Food Service. The exception, of course, is our Fresh Fish selection. As talked about earlier in this publication, Gordon Food Service has many Marketplace stores throughout the Midwest for you to be able to procure the same products we use at the Inn. Many dishes in this book call for fresh vegetables, and we recommend that those dishes be prepared seasonally as they are available in your locality, either from your own garden or a local market garden or farmer's market. Frozen ingredients are called for when they will not compromise quality, or when there are generally no fresh ingredients available.

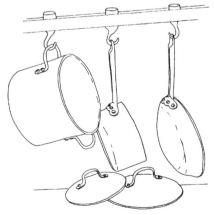

COOKWARE Three basic pans are used on top of the stove: the sauté pan, the saucepan and the soup pot. Generally, a skillet or frying pan is identical to a sauté pan. Where crepes are made, a crepe pan is preferred, but skillful use of a small sauté pan will suffice. In some cases, cast iron is called for—especially in blackening fish or meat—and any substitution would be ill-advised. Saucepans come in many sizes and differ from soup pots in the matter of handles. Both sauce pans and soup pots are cylindrical vessels with removable lids. Saucepans have a single long handle jutting out of one side, while soup pots have a pair of short handles attached to opposite sides of the pot. At the Inn, we prefer pots and pans that are round from the bottom to the sides, rather than those that have square transitions, as the rounded style is easier to clean thoroughly. Casserole and baking dishes are ovenproof dishes used to bake many recipes, and are used either covered or uncovered, as the recipe directs. Sheet pans are used for baking cookies and other desserts and some fish fillets. They are flat with low or no sides, and allow air circulated by a convection oven to move freely around the food being baked.

HERBS & SPICES The assumption in all recipes in this book is that fresh herbs and spices are used. Occasionally, dried herbs or spices are used and are so noted. If you wish to use dried herbs or spices where we have assumed that fresh will be used, it may be necessary to make adjustments to the quantity used to avoid varying the intensity of spicing.

TITCH Salt and pepper are generally used to taste. In many recipes, specific quantities will be called for and sometimes the amount needed is smaller than $1/8$ teaspoon (the smallest standard measure). In those cases, we have called for a titch, which is our measure for a quantity less than $1/8$ teaspoon, but more than nothing. A titch is smaller than a pinch.

PAPRIKA Several types of paprika are available, the most common being either Hungarian or Spanish. In these recipes, the use of Spanish paprika is assumed.

PARSLEY When fresh parsley is used, carefully wash, dry and finely chop, unless the recipe specifically calls for sprigs of parsley, in which case, carefully wash and dry but do not chop. It is particularly important that fresh parsley be carefully dried when making breadings and stuffings as excess moisture will upset the recipe.

GARLIC Many of these recipes call for garlic puree, which is a very convenient form of fresh garlic, and used extensively at the Inn. If you wish, you can substitute finely minced fresh garlic cloves.

ONIONS When dicing onions, always chop the onions by hand with a sharp knife rather than using a food processor. Processing onions draws moisture out of the onion; this moisture will make breadings too moist, and will spread onion flavor excessively in dishes like rice pilaf.

EGGS In all recipes, large eggs are assumed. If you wish to use medium-size eggs in recipes calling for three or more eggs, increase the number of eggs used.

FLOUR Whenever flour is called for, all-purpose is the type used. Many recipes call for flour that will be used to dredge some ingredients. The amount of flour called for is the quantity needed to work with in dredging—but is not meant to be entirely used up in the process. Some dredging flour will be left over, and if clean and dry may be saved for later use. If in doubt, discard remaining dredging flour.

ENCRUTE EnCrutes are anything baked in a pastry shell, generally poultry, meat or fish, though vegetable enCrutes are possible. Beef Wellington is perhaps the most well known EnCrute dish.

PASTA At the Inn, we use fresh pasta prepared in our kitchen. However, for these recipes we have not made the assumption that you will be preparing fresh pasta. If you can make your own, by all means do so. If fresh pasta is available from the local grocery or specialty food store, use that. If you use dried pasta, follow preparation instructions on the package carefully, and do not overcook.

IQF This stands for Individually Quick Frozen, and refers to a method of freezing fruit, shrimp and other foods. Many of the recipes that call for frozen fruit call for this type. It is available at GFS Marketplace stores and should be available in most grocery store freezer sections. We use IQF fruit because the individual pieces (in the case of cherries or raspberries, for example, individual fruits) are frozen separately, allowing you to remove from the freezer and use only what you need without thawing any excess. Also, the fruit does not have added sugar, and generally only the most attractive and best-flavored fruit is frozen in this manner.

LEMON Wrapped lemon halves are always served with fish and seafood entrées at the Inn. We have not included them in any ingredients list unless they are actually used in preparation, but we recommend the service of fresh lemon with fish and seafood entrées, particularly at a formal dinner party.

WOOKIES At the Inn, Cheese Wookies (Pg. 193) are served with every salad. We've included them here in the dessert section, as they are nice little cookies to serve as hor d'oevures with sparkling wine, or with fresh fruit for dessert, as well as to complement green salads.

SCROD VS SCHROD Debate rages in the culinary community about the proper spelling of this word. We've chosen to use Schrod, as it is John's favored spelling and is the one used by our purveyor, Steve Connolly Seafood. Note also that we've chosen to capitalize all fish names, making them stand out from surrounding text and making them easier to read.

STEAKS & FILLETS Fresh fish is sold in three principal ways: in the round, as steaks or as fillets. In the round is the whole fish, entrails removed, usually with the head and tail in place. A fish steak is a cut, usually of a large-sized fish that has had the entrails removed. The steak is a cross-section of the fish with back and rib bones removed. A fillet, on the other hand, is a cut that runs lengthwise from gills to tail on one side of the fish. It also does not include the back or rib bones, though in

30

some cases pin bones are still in fillets that are taken from three areas along the length of the fish—the head, middle and tail. Unless otherwise called for, the best fillets are from the tail, as they are likely to have the fewest bones.

PIN BONES It is sometimes necessary to remove the pin bones from fillets. Here's how. Place fillet skin-side down on a cutting board and run your finger along the top side of the thickest part of the fillet. This is where the pin bones, if still in the fillet, are located. You can feel the ends of the bones as you run your hand along the thick section of the fillet. To remove the bones, you will make a V-shaped cut, along the length of the fillet, centered on this line of bones. With a sharp knife, starting at the head end of the fillet about $1/8$ inch to the left of the pin bone line, cut about $3/4$ of the way through the fillet, angling right under the pin bones, and draw the knife down along the pin bone line to the tail end of the fillet. Make another cut, parallel to the first, beginning again at the head end of the fillet, this time 1/8 inch to the right of the pin bone line and angling left under the bones. The bottom of this cut should meet the bottom of the first cut. As you draw the knife down the line of the bones to the tail, you will produce a V-shaped cut that contains all the pin bones. This section of fish is then removed and discarded. The fillet is now de-boned and ready for further preparation.

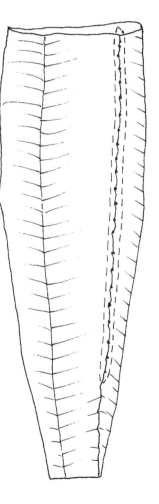

BREADINGS, STUFFINGS, SAUCES & DRESSINGS

"Animals are such agreeable friends -
they ask no questions, they pass no criticisms."

-George Elliot

Molly's Baby Biscuits

Yield   Lots

Ingredients

1 Jar	Chicken Baby Food
3/4 Cup	Low Fat Milk
1	Egg
3/4 Cup	Wheat Germ

Preparation

Preheat oven to 350 degrees. In a mixing bowl, combine all ingredients together and mix well. Using a sheet pan drop 1/2-tsp of batter with space between biscuits. Bake for 12 to 15 minutes and enjoy.

Hints

If you have not figured it out by the name of this recipe, this is a treat for your four legged family members. However, as you can see by the ingredients, all family members may enjoy.

Variations

Depending on the individual whims of this family member feel free to substitute beef, tuna, or whatever they desire.

CANTALOUPE SALSA ♣

YIELD	2 ¹/₂ CUPS

Cooks Notes

INGREDIENTS

2 Tbls	Brown Sugar
2 Cups	Cantaloupe - fresh, diced ◊
¹/₄ Cup	Mint - fresh chopped
¹/₄ Cup	Red Onion - diced fine
1	Lemon

PREPARATION

Prepare sets by removing the skin of 1 cantaloupe and cutting into a medium sized dice. With a sharp knife, chop fresh mint and dice red onion. Using a grater, grate the lemon creating the zest and squeeze out the juice. In a mixing bowl, combine all ingredients and lemon juice. With a spoon mix well and store in refrigeration.

HINTS

May be stored under refrigeration for three days.

VARIATIONS

◊ You may want to substitute Honeydew or any other solid melon.

USES

Used at the INN as a topping for the Marinated Halibut (pg 106). It is a great topping for any light fish entrée. Also makes a great garnish on any plate.

PROVENCALE SAUCE

Cooks Notes

YIELD   3 CUPS

INGREDIENTS

1/4 Cup	Olive Oil
6 oz	Garlic Clove
1/3 Cup	Onion - diced fine
1/3 Cup	Celery - diced fine
1 tsp	Oregano - fresh
1/4 Cup	Fresh Parsley - chopped
1 tsp	Basil - fresh
12	Tomatoes - medium size
1 Cup	Tomato Juice
3/4 Cup	White Wine
2 Tbls	Clam Base Δ
2 Gal	Water

PREPARATION

In a large saucepan, bring water to a boil. Add whole tomatoes and cook until skin splits. Remove from water and submerge in cold water to stop the cooking process. Drain water, remove skin, chop and set aside. With a sharp knife cut garlic cloves in half then, by placing the cut cloves between two plates, press the plates together pressing the garlic cloves, opening the pours in the garlic. Set aside. In a mixing bowl, combine white wine and clam base and mix thoroughly until clam base is dissolved. Set aside. In a medium size saucepan, over medium heat, heat olive oil until it becomes blue in color (very hot). Add garlic cloves and cook until golden brown (be very careful not to burn which results in a bitter taste). Remove cloves from oil. Add onions and celery and cook until translucent - about 4 minutes. Add oregano, parsley and basil. Cook over medium heat for 2 minutes. Add tomatoes, tomato juice, and clam base & wine mixture. Bring to a boil, reduce heat and simmer for 10 minutes. Be sure to stir frequently.

HINTS

◊ May be stored refrigerated for up to14 days.

VARIATIONS

Δ If clam base is not desired, chicken base is a good substitute.

USES

A great compliment for seafood, chicken, or as a topping on fresh vegetables. Also makes a great pizza sauce.

Cooks Notes

FRESH PESTO SAUCE ♣

Cooks Notes

YIELD   3 CUPS

INGREDIENTS

1 ¹/₂ Cups   Olive Oil
3 oz   Pine Nuts ◊
6 oz   Basil - fresh
1 Tbl   Garlic - chopped
8 oz   Parmesan Cheese - grated

PREPARATION
In a food processor, blend ¹/₂ cup olive oil with all other ingredients. Blend until smooth. While the processor is running add the balance of the olive oil.

HINTS
May be stored under refrigeration for up to 2 weeks.

VARIATIONS
◊ You may prefer to substitute walnuts or pecans.

FRESH SALSA ♣

YIELD   1 1/2 CUPS

Cooks Notes

INGREDIENTS

6	Tomatoes - diced
1/2	Red Onion - finely diced
1 Bunch	Scallions - chopped
1 Tbl	Garlic Puree
1	Jalapeno Pepper - finely diced
1 Tbl	Red Wine Vinegar
1 Tbl	Olive Oil
1/2 Bunch	Cilantro - chopped
1 tsp	Salt
1/2 tsp	Black Pepper

PREPARATION

Prepare sets by medium dicing tomatoes, fine dicing red onion, chopping scallions and cilantro. Remove the seeds from the Jalapeno pepper and finely dice. In a mixing bowl, combine all ingredients and mix completely. Refrigerate for at least 2 hours.

USES

Great as a garnish to any char grilled fish, chicken or as a topping to the Crab Meat & Avocado Quesadelli. (pg 68)

MUSTARD SAUCE ♣

YIELD   1 CUP

INGREDIENTS

3 Tbls	Butter - unsalted
1/2 Cup	White Wine - dry
1 Tbl	Tarragon - fresh chopped
2 tsp	Dijon Mustard
1/4 Cup	Heavy Cream
Titch	Salt
Titch	White Pepper

PREPARATION

Prepare set by chopping tarragon. In a medium saucepan, melt butter. Add wine, tarragon and mustard. Simmer until reduced by 1/2. Stirring constantly, pour in cream. Simmer for one minute. Ready to use.

USES

Sauce works well as a compliment to any broiled or char grilled ocean or fresh water fish, and topping a char grilled chicken breast.

Caesar Butter ♣

YIELD	1 Cup

INGREDIENTS

1/4 Lb	Butter - softened
1 Tbl	Caesar Fish Marinade (Pg 43)
1 tsp	Parmesan Cheese - grated

PREPARATION

Soften butter by allowing to-sit at room temperature for at least 2 hours. In a mixing bowl, combine butter, Caesar Fish Marinade and Parmesan cheese, mixing all ingredients together by hand. With your hands, form the mixture into a cylindrical log about 1 inch in diameter, roll up in parchment paper, twist the ends of the paper tight and store in a refrigerator Δ.

HINTS

Δ May be stored under refrigeration for up to one month. For longer term storage, rather than rolling the sauce in a piece of parchment paper, divide evenly into an ice cube tray, seal, and freeze; may be stored frozen for up to six months.

VARIATIONS

◊ A great topping for a baked potato or fresh green beans.

USES

Cut into 1/4-inch thick portions and place on top of char grilled entrees (meat, fish, or poultry) after cooking, just before serving.

MUSHROOM VELOUTÉ SAUCE

YIELD 2 ½ CUPS

INGREDIENTS

½ Cup	Mushrooms - sliced
2 Tbls	Shallots - minced
2 oz	Butter
1 oz	Flour
2 Cups	Chicken Stock Δ

PREPARATION

Prepare sets by washing and slicing mushrooms, peeling and fine mincing shallots. In a saucepan, bring chicken stock to a boil. In a sauté pan, over medium heat, melt 1 oz of butter and sauté mushrooms and shallots until tender. In a medium saucepan, over medium heat, melt 1 oz of butter, slowly stir in flour to make a roux. Cook for about 2 minutes, being careful not to burn. Slowly add (HOT) chicken stock and whip until smooth. Bring this sauce to a boil, then reduce heat to simmer. Add mushrooms and shallots and simmer for 10 minutes.

HINTS

Δ It is recommended that fresh chicken stock be used to produce the best results. However, a quality, canned product may be substituted.

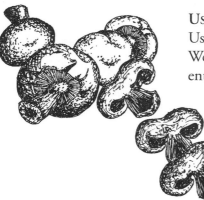

USES

Used at the INN as a sauce for Amy's Chicken Wellington (pg 144). Works well with pork and beef entrees as well.

CAESAR FISH MARINADE ♣

YIELD   1 ¹/₄ CUP

Cooks Notes

INGREDIENTS

³/₄ Cup	Olive Oil
¹/₄ Cup	Red Wine Vinegar
2 Tbls	Fresh Lemon Juice
1 Tbl	Dry Mustard
1 tsp	Salt
2 tsp	Black Pepper - ground

PREPARATION

In a mixing bowl, combine all ingredients. Place in a covered bowl and refrigerate. Best if made 24 hours prior to need.

HINTS

May be stored under refrigeration for up to one month

VARIATIONS

◊ Great for a dressing for potato salad, mixed green salad or green beans.

USES

Don't let the name fool you, also great as a marinade for steak, chicken, shrimp or pork.

RED WINE SHRIMP SAUCE

YIELD	4 CUPS

INGREDIENTS

2 oz	Shallots - diced
1/2 Cup	Shrimp - diced Δ1
5 oz	Butter
4 oz	Flour
4 oz	Red Wine
10 Cups	Chicken Stock Δ2

PREPARATION

Prepare shrimp by removing from the shell and cutting the shrimp in half lengthwise then crosscut to produce the diced form. Prepare shallots by peeling the skin and fine dicing. In a sauté pan, over medium heat, melt 1 oz of butter and sauté shallots and shrimp until shrimp obtains a pink color. Add red wine and simmer for 15 minutes. In a saucepan, bring chicken stock to a boil. In another saucepan, over medium heat, melt 4 oz of butter and slowly stir in flour to make a roux. Once hot (be careful not to burn), slowly stir in chicken stock. Whip until smooth. Fold in shrimp.

HINTS

Δ1 In the restaurant, we use what are called 21 x 25 Shrimp. This means 21-25 shrimp to the pound, and they are jumbo shrimp. You may find IQF (Individually Quick Frozen) shrimp with the shell on. Do not buy cooked shrimp. Δ2 It is recommended that fresh chicken stock be used to produce the best results. However, a quality, canned product may be substituted.

USES

Makes for a great topping for broiled or char grilled fish, pork or chicken entrees.

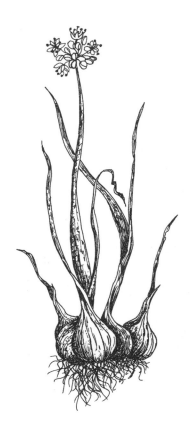

Horsey Sauce

Cooks Notes

YIELD   3 Cups

INGREDIENTS

1 Cup	Mayonnaise
1 Cup	Sour Cream
1 Cup	Horseradish
1 Tbl	Dijon Mustard

PREPARATION
In a mixing bowl, combine all ingredients, mix well and chill.

HINTS
May be stored under refrigeration for up to two weeks.

USES
A great compliment for vegetables, or wherever a little zing is needed to spice up a dish, like Prime Rib.

CHERRY VINAIGRETTE DRESSING ♣

YIELD   4 $^1/_2$ CUPS

INGREDIENTS

1 Cup	Cherry Vinegar Δ
2 Cups	Canola Oil
1 Cup	Maple Syrup
$^1/_4$ Cup	Country Dijon Mustard
$^1/_4$ Cup	Basil - fresh, chopped

PREPARATION
Mix all ingredients together well.

HINTS
May be stored, sealed under refrigeration for up to 1 month. It is always best to make dressings at least one day ahead of use to allow the flavors to marry.
Δ Cherry vinegar is available in most food specialty shops. However, should you wish to make your own, combine 2 cups white vinegar and 2 cups red wine vinegar and add 3 cups of tart cherries cut in $^1/_2$ and allow it to stand for 36 hours. Then strain.

USES
Use as a salad dressing or as a fine fish, poultry or meat marinade. A great recommendation for grilled shrimp or sea scallops.

CHERRY PUNGENT FRUIT SAUCE

Cooks Notes

YIELD   1 ¼ CUPS

INGREDIENTS

1 - 15.5oz jar	Cherry Preserves ◊
1 Tbls	Horseradish
1 Tbl	Fresh Lemon Juice
1 tsp	Dry Mustard
1 tsp	Ginger - ground
⅛ tsp	Tabasco Sauce

PREPARATION

Combine all ingredients in a blender and blend for
15 - 20 seconds. Serve at room temperature or chilled.

HINTS

May be stored under refrigeration for up to 3 weeks. We
do not recommend freezing this sauce.

VARIATIONS

◊ Various preserves or marmalades may be substituted to
change the character of the sauce.

USES

This sauce is a fine accompaniment to poultry entrees,
pork tenderloin and Grilled Shrimp (pg. 124). Also use
atop cream cheese as a cracker spread.

DEMI GLAZE CREAM SAUCE

YIELD   1 CUP

INGREDIENTS

2 oz   Demi Glaze - prepared
8 oz   Water - hot
1/4 Cup   Heavy Cream
              Salt & Pepper to taste

PREPARATION
For home use it is much easier to use a prepared Demi Glaze versus the time and energy necessary to do a full stock reduction. GFS has such a product available. In a saucepan, over medium heat, stir in Demi Glaze until dissolved. When completely dissolved turn off heat and whisk in the whipping cream. Keep warm, ready to use.

USES
Great as a topping for wild mushrooms, and char grilled meats.

PRIMAVERA SAUCE ♣

YIELD   3 CUPS

Cooks Notes

INGREDIENTS

2 Cups	Olive Oil
1 Tbl	Garlic - minced
3/4 Cup	Water - hot
2 Tbls	Clam Base ◊
1/4 Cup	Fresh Parsley - chopped

PREPARATION

Using a blender, add 1-cup olive oil and garlic and blend. In a mixing bowl, combine hot water and clam base mixing well until clam base is dissolved, set aside. In a saucepan, over high heat, add 1-cup olive oil and heat to very hot. Add blended garlic mixture to hot oil and remove from heat. Add in chopped parsley then clam base mixture and mix well.

HINTS

◊ To refrain from a seafood flavor, substitute chicken base for clam base.

USES

May be stored refrigerated up to 3 weeks. A great sauce to sauté fresh vegetables, shrimp, scallops or light meats as an appetizer or as a base for a pasta dish, HOT or chilled.

HERB CREAM SAUCE

YIELD   1 1/4 CUP

INGREDIENTS

1/4 Cup	Butter
1 Cup	Mushrooms - fine chopped
2 Large	Shallots - chopped
3	Garlic Cloves - finely chopped
2 tsp	Flour
3/4 Cup	Heavy Cream
1/4 Cup	Dry Vermouth
2 tsp	Fresh Lemon Juice
1/2 tsp	Oregano - fresh, chopped
1/2 tsp	Basil - fresh, chopped
1/4 tsp	Thyme - fresh, chopped
1 tsp	Black Pepper - ground
1 Tbl	Fresh Parsley - chopped
1 tsp	Capers

PREPARATION

Prepare sets by chopping fine, garlic, shallots, mushrooms, oregano, basil, thyme and parsley and set aside. In a saucepan, over medium heat, melt butter, add mushroom, shallots and garlic and cook until tender. Add flour and mix completely. Cook for 3 minutes not stirring. Add cream, vermouth, lemon juice, oregano, basil, thyme and pepper. Continue cooking over medium heat until mixture thickens. Add capers and parsley.

USES

Sauce works well as a compliment to any broiled ocean or fresh water fish, and topping a char grilled chicken breast.

Steak Marinade ♣

YIELD	4 Cups

Cooks Notes

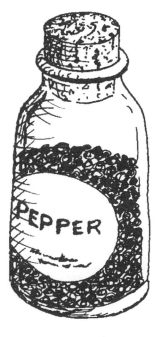

INGREDIENTS

1/2 Cup	Black Pepper - cracked
1/2 Cup	Molasses
1 1/2 Cups	Balsamic Vinegar ◊
1/2 Cup	Garlic - chopped
1 Cup	Olive Oil
1/2 Cup	Dijon Mustard

PREPARATION
Prepare sets by chopping fresh garlic into a fine chop. In a food processor, combine all ingredients and blend to a puree. Store in a covered container refrigerated.

HINTS
Δ1 May be stored under refrigeration for up to one month. Once marinade is used however, it should be discarded. Δ2 Meats should be marinated for at least 6 hours.

VARIATIONS
◊ Red wine vinegar or flavored vinegars may be substituted.

HOT BACON SAUCE 🐖

Cooks Notes

YIELD   3 CUPS

INGREDIENTS

1/4 Lb	Onion - finely chopped
1/2 Lb	Bacon - finely chopped
1 Cup	Water
1 Cup	White Vinegar
1/4 Lb	Sugar
1/2 Tbl	Salt
1/2 tsp	White Pepper - ground
1 oz	Corn Starch
1/2 Cup	Water

PREPARATION

In a sauté pan, fry bacon and onions together until onions are clear and bacon is crisp. Drain the drippings and save. In a saucepan, combine water and vinegar, boil and add sugar, salt and pepper. In a mixing bowl, combine corn starch, water and drippings from bacon. Mix together, forming a smooth paste. Stir this mixture into the boiling water, and mix until slightly thickened. Cook about 10 minutes. Add onions and bacon.

HINTS

May be stored under refrigeration for up to one month.

USES

A great dressing for wilted spinach salad. Also used as a topping for items with Florentine stuffing.

COCKTAIL SAUCE ♣

YIELD   1 CUP

Cooks Notes

INGREDIENTS

1/2 Cup	Ketchup
1/2 Cup	Chili Sauce
1 1/2 Tbls	Horseradish
1 1/2 Tbls	Fresh Lemon Juice
1 tsp	Worcestershire Sauce

PREPARATION

In a mixing bowl, combine all ingredients. Whip until
well blended and chill for at least 2 hours prior to use.

PEPPERADA SAUCE ♣

YIELD   12 CUPS

INGREDIENTS

8 Lrg	Ripe Garden Tomatoes
1 Tbl	Capers - chopped
1 Cup	Basil - fresh, chopped
2 Tbls	Oregano - fresh, chopped
1 1/2 Cups	Canola Oil
3 Cups	Provencale Sauce (pg 36)
4 Tbls	Lemon Pepper
3 Cups	Parmesan Cheese - grated

PREPARATION

Place tomatoes in a pot and cover with water. Bring to a boil and cook until tomato skins begin to split. Remove tomatoes from hot water and plunge into a cold water bath. Peel skins from tomatoes, then course chop tomatoes. In a large mixing bowl, combine all ingredients and mix completely. Refrigerate at least 1 hour prior to use.

USES

A great sauce for a spicy pasta dish.

MOULIN ROUGE SAUCE ♣

YIELD   2 ½ CUPS

Cooks Notes

INGREDIENTS

1 Cup	Heavy Cream
¾ Cup	Chili Sauce
½ Cup	Chives - fresh, minced
2 tsps	Sour Cream
2 tsps	Worchestshire Sauce
1 Tbl	Oregano - fresh, chopped
1 Tbl	Basil - fresh, chopped
1 tsp	Tabasco Sauce

PREPARATION

Prepare sets by chopping chives, oregano and basil. In a mixing bowl, combine all ingredients and mix well. Refrigerate for at least 1 hour.

HINTS

May be stored under refrigeration for up to 7 days.

VARIATIONS

◊ Vary the amount of Tabasco sauce to change the intensity of flavor.

USES

It is a nice compliment to any full flavored or blackened fish or meat.

GREAT BEGINNINGS

"If you do what you've always done, you'll get what you've always gotten."

-Moms Mabley

WHITNEY'S LIVER SNAPS

YIELD   LOTS

INGREDIENTS

3 Lbs	Beef or Chicken Liver
1 1/2 Lbs	Wheat Germ
1 Cup	Corn Meal
1/2 Cup	Parmesan Cheese - grated
4	Eggs
1	Garlic Clove

PREPARATION

Preheat oven at 350 degrees. Combine all ingredients in a food processor and blend for 5 minutes. On a greased sheet pan, evenly spaced, put 1 Tbl dollops of batter and bake for 20 minutes. Remove from oven and completely cool prior to serving.

HINTS

If you have not figured it out by the name of this recipe, this is a treat for your four legged family members. However, as you can see by the ingredients, all family members may enjoy.

STUFFED PORTABELLA MUSHROOM CAPS

Cooks Notes

YIELD   4 SERVINGS

INGREDIENTS

1 Cup	Olive Oil
1/2 Cup	Balsamic Vinegar
4	Portabella Caps
2 Cups	Mushroom - diced ◊1
4 Slices	Bacon
1 Tbl	Garlic - chopped
1 tsp	Rosemary - fresh, chopped
1/4 Cup	Kalamata Olives - chopped ◊2
2 oz	Cream Cheese - softened
4 oz	Lemon Butter Sauce (pg 196)
2 Tbls	Fresh Parsley - chopped

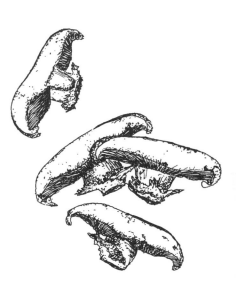

PREPARATION

Chop parsley and set aside. Set out cream cheese to soften. In a mixing bowl, combine olive oil and balsamic vinegar, to make marinade. Marinate mushroom caps for 4 hours. Preheat char grill. Prepare sets by fine dicing mushrooms, chopping fresh garlic, fresh rosemary and olives. Remove caps from marinade and char grill, top down, over medium heat until slightly soft, 3-4 minutes. Set aside to cool. Preheat oven to 375 degrees. In a large sauté pan, over medium heat, cook bacon until crisp. Using tongs, transfer bacon to paper towel and drain. Pour off all but 1 Tbl of bacon drippings from sauté pan. Add chopped mushrooms, garlic, rosemary and sauté over medium heat until tender - about 10 minutes. Crumble bacon and add to skillet. Add olives and mix well. In a mixing bowl, whip cream cheese until smooth. Add mushroom mixture and mix completely. Place Portabella mushroom cap-side down on sheet pan and divide mushroom mixture evenly into the cavity of the cap. Bake for 15 minutes. Remove and top with Lemon Butter Sauce, chopped parsley and serve.

VARIATIONS

◊1 Morels, Shittaki or any preferred mushroom works in this recipe. ◊2 Ripe black olives may be substituted.

LCI HERB BREAD

Cooks Notes

YIELD   4 LOAVES

INGREDIENTS

1 Pkg	Dry Yeast
1 1/2 Cups	Water
1 Tbl	Sugar
1 Tbl	Salt
2 Tbls	Olive Oil
4 Cups	High Gluten Flour
1/4 Cup	Kosher Salt
2 Tbls	Poppy Seed

Topping
1 Cup	Olive Oil
2 Tbls	Oregano - fresh, chopped
1/8 tsp	Salt
1 oz	Garlic Puree

PREPARATION
Dough
Preheat Oven to 425 degrees. In an electric mixing bowl, combine warm water (115 degrees) and yeast. After yeast dissolves add sugar, salt and oil, mixing well. On low speed, add flour and mix until dough becomes smooth and soft and leaves the sides of the bowl, remove dough and knead by hand 3-4 minutes. Set aside in a warm area and allow dough to rise until doubled in size. In a mixing bowl, combine kosher salt and poppy seeds and set aside. Separate dough into 4 equal portions and roll into a long loaf shape. Sprinkle the bread with the kosher salt, poppy seed mixture. Line a sheet pan with parchment paper and place loaves on the pan leaving space in between loaves. With a pair of scissors, on a 45-degree angle, make cuts evenly spaced in the bread depending on the size roll you desire and cut $^3/_4$ of the way through. Separate pieces by twisting each roll outward. Δ1 Brush on topping and bake for 15 minutes or until golden brown.

Topping
In a mixing bowl, combine all ingredients and mix vigorously.

HINTS
Δ1 May be stored covered and refrigerated up to 24 hours. If bread is stored refrigerated, remove and bring to room temperature prior to baking.

VARIATIONS
Left over baked bread can be cut in $^1/_2$ inch cubes and used as croutons for salads

Cooks Notes

WILD MUSHROOM CHEESECAKE

YIELD   16 SERVINGS

INGREDIENTS

Crust
1 Cup	Parmesan Cheese - grated
1/2 Cup	Pecans - chopped
1 Cup	Bread Crumbs
3/4 Cup	Butter - softened

Batter
1 Cup	Green Onions - chopped
1 Cup	Red or Yellow Peppers - chopped
2 Cups	Morels Mushrooms - dried, chopped
2 Cups	Porcini Mushrooms - dried, chopped
2 tsp	Salt
1 tsp	Pepper
2 Tbls	Basil - fresh, chopped
2 Lbs	Cream Cheese - softened
4	Eggs
1/2 Cup	Heavy Cream
1 Lb	Crab Meat
1 Cup	Fresh Pesto Sauce (pg 38)
1 Cup	Smoked Gouda Cheese - shredded

PREPARATION

Set butter and cream cheese out at room temperature to soften. Prepare sets by chopping green onions, and peppers. In a saucepan, bring water to a boil and cook Porcini and Morels for 20 minutes. Drain, chop and set aside.

Crust

In a food processor, combine Parmesan cheese, pecans, breadcrumbs and 1/2 cup of butter. Mix thoroughly. Press crust into a 9-inch spring form pan.
Preheat oven to 350 degrees.

Batter

In a sauté pan, melt 1/4 cup of butter and sauté onions, peppers, mushrooms, salt, pepper and basil. In a food processor, whip cream cheese and eggs together until well mixed, about 5 minutes. Then add cream & Gouda and mix completely. Add vegetables and mix well. Pour filling into spring form pan and bake for 1 hour, 15 minutes. Remove from oven and completely cool prior to serving. Portion cheesecake and plate and top each portion with 2 Tbls of Pesto Sauce.

Mini Whitefish Neptune

YIELD   4 SERVINGS

INGREDIENTS

4 - 5 oz	Whitefish Fillets Δ ◊1
1 Cup	Crab Meat Stuffing (pg 207)
1/2 tsp	Paprika
1/2 tsp	Canola Oil
1/2 Cup	Béarnaise Sauce (pg 206) ◊2
2 Tbls	Fresh Parsley - chopped

PREPARATION

Chop parsley and set aside. If necessary, remove pin bones from fillets, (see Pg 31 for instructions). Preheat oven to 350 degrees. Place the fillets on a baking pan. Lay 1/4 cup Crab Meat Stuffing on the top of each fillet and shape to the fillet, covering about 3/4 of the fillet. Press the stuffing into place and sprinkle fillet and stuffing with paprika. Brush oil on the stuffed fillets and bake for 12 minutes. Remove from oven. Arrange fillets on a serving platter and top each with 2 Tbls Béarnaise Sauce. Sprinkle chopped parsley on fillets and serve.

HINTS

Δ The importance of quality fish cannot be over emphasized. The difference between a superb fish dinner and an ordinary dinner begins with the quality of the fish.

VARIATIONS

◊1 If fresh whitefish is not available, several fresh lake and ocean fish are excellent stuffed and baked including Lake Trout, Pickerel, Salmon, Schrod, and Sole. ◊2 Instead of Béarnaise Sauce, Lemon Butter Sauce (pg 196) with or without pecans may be used.

CRAB CAKES

YIELD   **8 SERVINGS**

Cooks Notes

INGREDIENTS

1 Lb	Lump Crab Meat Δ
1	Egg
5 Tbls	Mayonnaise
1 Tbl	Fresh Parsley - chopped
2 tsp	Worcestershire Sauce
1 tsp	Prepared Mustard
1 tsp	Salt
1/4 tsp	White Pepper - ground
1/2 Cup	Bread Crumbs
2 Tbls	Olive Oil
4 Tbls	Lemon Butter Sauce (pg 196)
2 Tbls	Fresh Parsley - chopped

PREPARATION

Chop parsley and set aside. Preheat oven to 375 degrees. In a mixing bowl, combine egg, mayonnaise, 1 Tbl chopped parsley, Worcestershire sauce, mustard, salt and pepper. Mix well. Gently fold in crab meat being careful not to break apart. Refrigerate for at least 1 hour. Equally divide mixture into 8 portions and pat out to make cakes - about 3/4-inch thick. Place cakes on a sheet pan and bake for 12 minutes. Remove and top with Lemon Butter Sauce, chopped parsley and serve.

HINTS

Δ It is recommended that genuine Maryland lump crab meat be used. When using this product, however, be sure to drain and remove any shell.

USES

Makes a great sandwich between 2 slices of a good sour dough bread or Kaiser roll.

BOURSIN CHEESE

YIELD   4 SERVINGS

INGREDIENTS

1-5oz	Boursin Cheese
1 Cup	Provencale Sauce (pg 36)
8	Whole Caper Berries
30 Slices	French Bread - 2 inch diameter
$^1/_2$ Cup	Garlic Butter Sauce (pg 197)
2 Tbls	Fresh Parsley - chopped

PREPARATION

Preheat oven to 350 degrees. Chop parsley and set aside. Prepare Provencale Sauce per recipe. Prepare Garlic Butter Sauce per recipe. Cut the French bread on a 45 degree angle about $^1/_2$ inch thick and brush with the Garlic Butter Sauce and broil for 1-2 minutes, being careful not to burn. Cut Boursin in half, cross-wise creating a half moon shape. Equally divide Provencale Sauce into two small casserole dishes place Boursin, cut-side down in the center of the dish. Place Caper Berries north, south, east and west around cheese. Bake for 10 minutes. Remove from oven. Sprinkle with chopped parsley. Place each casserole dish in the center of a serving plate, surround with toast points and serve.

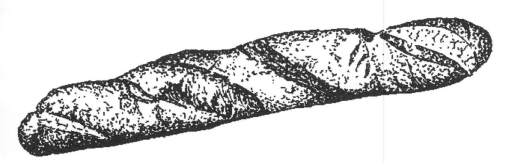

ASIAGO CHEESE CROSTINI

YIELD   12 SERVINGS

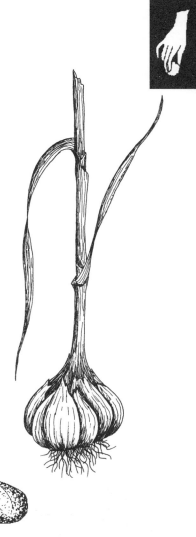

INGREDIENTS

¹/₂ Loaf	French Bread
¹/₂ Cup	Basil - fresh, chopped
¹/₂ Cup	Garden Ripe Tomato - chopped
2 tsp	Garlic Puree
15	Kalamata Olives - chopped ◊1
¹/₄ Cup	Asiago Cheese ◊2

PREPARATION
Slice bread ¹/₄-inch thick. In a mixing bowl, combine all other ingredients and mix well. Spread ¹/₂ Tbl of mixture on each slice of bread and broil until cheese is hot and melted - about 2 minutes.

VARIATIONS
◊1 Pitted ripe olives may be substituted. ◊2 Any aged sharp white cheese works well with this recipe.

USES
This is great for a light appetizer.

CRAB AND AVOCADO QUESADILLA

YIELD	16 SERVINGS

INGREDIENTS

¹/₂ Lb	Lump Crab Meat Δ
1	Ripe Avocado - diced
2 Tbls	Sour Cream
1	Jalapeno Pepper - diced
1	Lemon - zest
1	Lime - zest
¹/₄ Cup	Cilantro - chopped
4 Tbls	Olive Oil
4	Flour Tortillas
¹/₂ Cup	Monterey Jack Cheese - grated

PREPARATION

Prepare sets by dicing avocado, pepper, and chopping Cilantro. Grate lemon and lime creating the zest. In a mixing bowl, combine crab, avocado, sour cream, pepper, zest and Cilantro. Mix carefully so as not to break up the crab meat. Salt and pepper to taste. In a sauté pan, heat oil until it is hot. Sauté each tortilla for 10 seconds on each side. Set them on a paper towel to absorb oil. Spread ¹/₄ of the mixture on ¹/₂ of the tortillas and fold them over. Place the filled, folded tortillas on a baking sheet pan. Sprinkle the cheese on top and broil until the cheese melts. Be careful not to burn. Cut each tortilla into 4 triangles and serve.

HINTS

Δ It is recommended that genuine Maryland lump crab meat is used. When using this product, however, be sure to drain and remove any shell.

VARIATIONS

Top with Fresh Salsa (pg. 39) to add color and flavor.

GARLIC SHRIMP

YIELD   4 SERVINGS

Cooks Notes

INGREDIENTS

20	Jumbo Shrimp Δ
1 Cup	Flour
$^1/_2$ Cup	Olive Oil
1 Cup	Garlic Butter Sauce (pg 197)
$^1/_4$ Cup	Sliced Almonds - toasted
2 Tbls	Fresh Parsley - chopped

PREPARATION

Chop parsley and set aside. Remove shrimp from the shell Δ2 and lay on side. Butterfly the shrimp by carefully inserting a sharp knife into the large end of the shrimp, cutting in about $^3/_4$ of the way to the back, then cutting to the tail. Be careful not to cut through the shrimp. Rinse the shrimp clean and set aside. Spread almonds on a sheet pan and broil for 2 minutes or until golden brown, being careful not to burn. Hold shrimp by the tail and place on a baking sheet pan. Arrange shrimp tightly in rows and brush them with olive oil. Evenly distribute Garlic Butter Sauce over the shrimp. Wrap and refrigerate for at least 1 hour. Preheat broiler and cook shrimp approximately 4 minutes on each side until the Garlic Butter Sauce and shrimp are lightly browned. Place shrimp on a serving platter and garnish with toasted almonds and chopped parsley.

HINTS

Δ1 In the restaurant, we use what are called 21 x 25 Shrimp. This means 21-25 shrimp to the pound, and they are jumbo shrimp. Another common size is 15 x 20 a bit larger, and as good for this recipe. You may find IQF (individually Quick Frozen) shrimp with the shell on. Do not buy cooked shrimp. If you find E-Z Peel shrimps, buy them - they have been cleaned and the shell will pull off easily, and are worth the extra cost. Δ2 For the most professional looking dish, carefully leave tail on the shrimp when removing from the shell.

SMOKED SALMON WITH RED RADISH DILL SAUCE

Cooks Notes

YIELD	4 SERVINGS

INGREDIENTS

10 oz	Smoked Salmon - sliced
1 tsp	Wasabi Powder
2 tsp	Water
8 oz	Celery Root - diced
3 oz	Sour Cream
2	Chive Strings

Red Radish Dill Sauce

1/2 Cup	Dry White Wine
1/2 Cup	Heavy Cream
1	Shallot - finely chopped
1 Cup	Butter - unsalted
1/4 tsp	White Pepper
1/2 tsp	Salt
8 Lrg	Red Radish
3 Tbls	Dill - fresh, chopped
1 Tbl	Horseradish
2 Tbls	Fresh Parsley - chopped

PREPARATION

Chop parsley and set aside. Form the slices of smoked
salmon into 4 rectangles. Remove any trimmings for the
stuffing. In a mixing bowl, dilute the Wasabi powder
with 2 tsp of water. Mix the celery root with the sour
cream, diluted Wasabi and any salmon trimmings. Place
equal portions of stuffing on each salmon rectangle. Roll
the piece of salmon securing the stuffing in place. Using
a chive 'string' tie off each end of the roll.

Red Radish Dill Sauce
Prepare set by finely chopping shallot, washing and
trimming radishes, and chopping dill. Cut butter into
1-inch cubes. Cut 12 thin slices from the radishes, finely
chopping the rest. Over medium heat, sauté the wine,
cream and shallot. Heat to a boil and cook over medium
heat until reduced to $1/2$ cup - about 10 minutes. Reduce
heat to low and whisk in butter, 1 cube at a time. Season
with white pepper and salt and remove sauce from heat.
Add radishes, dill and horseradish to the sauce.

To Finish
Place a pool of red radish sauce in the center of the
dinner plate and rest 1 salmon roll on the sauce. Garnish
with fresh parsley and serve.

Cooks Notes

SOUPS,
SALADS &
SIDE DISHES

"There is nothing which has yet been
contrived by man, by which so
much happiness is produced as
by a good tavern or inn."

-Samuel Johnson

SOUTHERN SPINACH SALAD ♣

YIELD	8 SERVINGS

INGREDIENTS

1 Lb.	Baby Spinach
1 Head	Lettuce - ◊1
2 Cups	Mandarin Oranges - sections
1 Cup	Peanuts - dry roasted
1 Cup	Artichoke Hearts - drained, quartered
1 Cup	Kalamata Olives ◊2
1/2 Lb	Swiss Cheese - shredded
4	Green Onions - diced
1/3 Cup	Sugar
1 Tbl	Dry Mustard
1 Tbl.	Salt
1/8 tsp.	Black Pepper - ground
1 Tbl	Celery Seed
1 Tbl	Onion - grated
1/3 Cup	Red Wine Vinegar
1 Cup	Canola Salad Oil

PREPARATION

Drain mandarin oranges and separate into sections and set aside. Drain artichoke hearts and quarter, set aside. Cut spinach and lettuce into $1/4$ inch pieces. Combine spinach and lettuce with oranges, peanuts, artichokes, olives, cheese and green onion. Δ In a mixing bowl, combine sugar, dry mustard, salt, pepper, celery seed and grated onion. Add vinegar and oil and mix vigorously. Add dressing to salad mixture and fold gently. Ready to serve.

Cooks Notes

HINTS

Δ Dressing should be chilled for at least 2 hours prior to serving.

VARIATIONS

◊1 Any lettuce such as Leaf, Red Leaf, Romaine, or Bibb may be substituted for Head Lettuce. ◊2 Ripe or Greek Olives may be substituted.

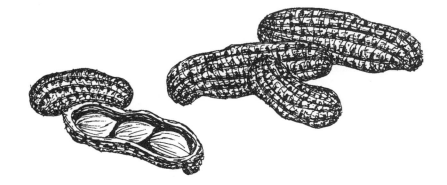

TORTELLINI SALAD ♣

YIELD   **6 SERVINGS**

INGREDIENTS

10 oz	Fresh Cheese Tortellini
1/4 Cup	Fresh Parsley - finely chopped
1/4 Lb	Havarti Cheese - cubed
1	Red Pepper - chopped
1/2 Cup	Black Olives - sliced
2	Green Onions

Dressing	
3 Tbls	Red Wine Vinegar
1 Tbl	Basil - fresh
1 tsp	Dijon Mustard
1/4 tsp	Salt
1/4 tsp	Black Pepper - coarse grind
1	Garlic Clove - minced
1/2 Cup	Olive Oil

PREPARATION

Dressing

In a blender combine all dressing ingredients and blend well. Refrigerate for at least 1 hour.

In a saucepan, boil Tortellini until al dente, then drain. Prepare sets by chopping parsley, cubing Havarti, chopping pepper, slicing olives and slicing the entire green onions, tops included. In a large bowl, combine Tortellini, parsley, cheese, pepper, olives, and green onions. Mix chilled dressing and then pour over the Tortellini, folding to mix completely without breaking apart the Tortellini. Refrigerate this dish at least 1 hour prior to serving.

HINTS

If you are making Tortellini more than 1 hour ahead of serving then hold back half of the dressing for folding into chilled Tortellini dish. Make a more substantial salad by adding chicken or shrimp.

Salad Leelanau ♣

Yield	4 Servings

Ingredients

1 Head	Bibb Lettuce - large
1 Head	Red Boston Bibb - large
4 Tbls	Pecans - chopped, toasted
4 Tbls	Gorgonzola Cheese
3 Tbls	Dried Cherries
1/2 Cup	Cherry Vinaigrette Dressing (pg 46)

Preparation

Prepare pecans by chopping and then under a hot broiler, toast for 2 minutes or until golden brown. Chill large salad bowl. Wash and dry the lettuces Δ. Hand-tear the lettuces into the large salad bowl and mix well. Sprinkle pecans, cheese, and dried cherries on the lettuces. At the table, before serving, toss with Cherry Vinaigrette Dressing.

Hints

Δ Dressings will not stick to wet lettuce. Always be certain the lettuce is dry by draining for several hours or spinning dry, and carefully patting with a dry towel.

BERNA'S SPINACH CASSEROLE

YIELD   8 SERVINGS

INGREDIENTS

1 Pkg	Corn Muffin Mix - (6 - 8^1/$_2$oz)
2	Eggs - beaten
1 Cup	Sour Cream
1 10oz Can	French Onion Soup - Δ1
1 10oz Pkg	Spinach - chopped
^{1}/$_2$ Cup	Butter - melted
^{1}/$_2$ Cup	Sharp Cheddar Cheese - grated

PREPARATION

Preheat oven to 350 degrees. Squeeze spinach dry Δ2.
Chop and set aside. In a mixing bowl, combine corn
muffin mix, eggs, sour cream, onion soup, spinach and
butter. Mix well and place in a 12x8x2 baking dish,
greased. Bake at 350 degrees for 25 minutes. Remove
and top with grated sharp cheese and bake an additional
5 minutes.

HINTS

Δ1 Onion Soup should not be diluted with water.
Δ2 It is important that the spinach be as dry as possible,
as excessive moisture results in a casserole that will not
hold together. To dry spinach, place the spinach in the
center of a kitchen towel, bring up the sides and twist
the cloth to squeeze out excess moisture.

GAZPACHO ♣

YIELD	6 SERVINGS

Cooks Notes

INGREDIENTS

1 Large	Cucumber - finely diced
1/2	Green Pepper - finely diced
1/2	Red Pepper - finely diced
1/2	Yellow Pepper - finely diced
1/2 Large	Onion - finely diced
3 Tbls	Fresh Parsley - finely chopped
2 Tbls	Basil - fresh, finely chopped
1	Garlic Clove - minced
1 Cup	Greek Dressing (pg 210)
6 Large	Garden Ripe Tomatoes - course chop
1 Cup	Tomato Juice
6 Tbls	Sour Cream

PREPARATION

Prepare sets by chopping, dicing and mincing where indicated. Peel tomatoes prior to dicing. In a mixing bowl, combine cucumbers, peppers, onion, parsley, basil and garlic, mixing well. Add in Greek dressing, tomatoes, salt and pepper to taste and chill at least 2 hours prior to serving. Serve in a goblet and garnish with a Tbl of sour cream.

HINTS

May be stored under refrigeration for up to 3 days.

GARLIC MASHED POTATOES

Cooks Notes

YIELD   20 SERVINGS

INGREDIENTS

6 Lbs	Potatoes - peeled, diced
1 Gal	Water
3/4 Cup	Heavy Cream
3/4 Cup	Half & Half
1/3 Lb	Butter - softened
10	Garlic Cloves
1/8 Cup	Olive Oil
1/4 Tbl	Black Pepper
3/4 Tbl	Salt

PREPARATION
Preheat oven to 425 degrees.

Roasting Garlic
Peel garlic cloves and rub with olive oil. Place garlic in a shallow pan with garlic submerged about 1/4 of the way in water. Bake for 25 minutes covered. Remove the cover and bake an additional 20 minutes. In a soup pot, bring 1 gallon of water to a boil and add diced potatoes and cook for 5 minutes, at a rolling boil. Turn off heat and let sit in water for an additional 5 minutes. Drain potatoes and place into a mixer. Mix well at low speed, removing all lumps. Add heavy cream, half & half, butter, roasted garlic, black pepper and salt. Mix well. Ready to serve.

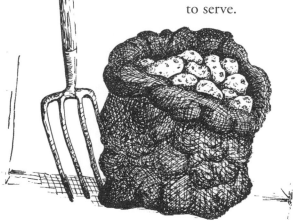

OYSTER BISQUE

YIELD	4 SERVINGS

Cooks Notes

INGREDIENTS

1 Qt	Select Oysters
1	Bay Leaf
2	Onions - medium chopped
3	Celery Stalks - chopped
1/2 Cup	Butter
1/4 Cup	Flour
1/2 tsp	Salt
1/4 tsp	White Pepper - ground
1 Cup	Heavy Cream
1/4 Cup	Dry Sherry
1/4 Cup	Fresh Parsley - chopped

PREPARATION

Chop parsley and set aside. Drain oysters, saving juice. Medium chop oysters and set aside. In a medium soup pot, add enough water to oyster juice to yield 2 quarts. Over high heat add bay leaf, 1 chopped onion and 1 chopped celery stalk. Simmer uncovered 30 minutes. Remove from heat and let stand for 1 hour, then strain. In a saucepan, melt butter, get hot and add remaining onion and celery. Sauté until soft and translucent. Stir in flour, but do not allow to brown. Remove from heat and add half the oyster liquid stock stirring constantly. Return to heat and add remaining oyster stock. Stir until smooth. Add salt and pepper and cook gently over low heat for 10 minutes. Add oysters and cream and simmer 3 additional minutes. Stir in sherry just before serving. Garnish with fresh parsley.

PASTA
AT THE INN

"The best way to get the better of temptation
is just to yield to it."

-Clementina Stirling Graham

SEAFOOD PROVENCALE ♣

Cooks Notes

YIELD   6 SERVINGS

INGREDIENTS

4 Cups	Provencale Sauce (pg 36)
12 oz	Shrimp Δ1
12 oz	Cape Scallops
1¹/₂ Lbs	Pasta ◊1
2 Tbls	Fresh Parsley - chopped

PREPARATION

Chop parsley and set aside. Prepare the Provencale Sauce per recipe. Remove shrimp from the shell Δ2 and lay on side. Butterfly the shrimp by carefully inserting sharp knife into the large end of the shrimp, cutting in about 3/4 of the way to the back, then cutting to the tail. Be careful not to cut through the shrimp. Rinse the shrimp, set aside. Prepare pasta according to package directions, drain, and keep warm. In a large sauté pan, over high heat add the Provencale sauce, scallops and shrimp and cook until shrimp is pink in color, about 3 minutes. Add mixture to cooked pasta and fold, mixing well. Divide evenly on 6 plates top with chopped parsley and serve.

HINTS

Δ1 In the restaurant, we use what are called 21 x 25 Shrimp. This means 21-25 shrimp to the pound, and they are jumbo shrimp. Another common size is 15 x 20 a bit larger, and as good for this recipe. You may find IQF (individually Quick Frozen) shrimp with the shell on. Do not buy cooked shrimp. If you find E-Z Peel shrimps, buy them - they have been cleaned and the shell will pull off easily, and are worth the extra cost. Δ2 For the most professional looking dish, carefully leave tail on the shrimp when removing from the shell.

VARIATIONS

◊1 Any style pasta noodle works with this recipe.

SUGGESTED WINES

Dry, light or medium white:
Good Harbor Chardonnay

OR

Semi-dry, light or medium White:
Good Harbor Trillium

SUGGESTED DINNER MENU

Garlic Shrimp (pg 69)

Salad Leelanau (pg 77)

Seafood Provencale

White Chocolate Cake & Raspberry Sauce (pg 178)

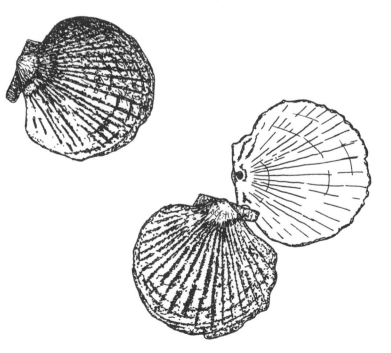

GREEK SHRIMP ♣

Cooks Notes

YIELD   4 SERVINGS

INGREDIENTS

1¹/₂ Cup	Primavera Sauce (pg 49)
24	Jumbo Shrimp - shell on Δ1
4 Tbl	Basil - fresh, chopped
4 Tbl	Oregano - fresh, chopped
1 Cup	Tomatoes - fresh, diced
2 Cup	Feta cheese - crumbled
2 Cup	Pasta ◊
2 Tbls	Fresh Parsley - chopped

PREPARATION

Chop parsley and set aside. Prepare the Primavera Sauce per recipe. Remove shrimp from the shell Δ2 and lay on side. Butterfly the shrimp by carefully inserting sharp knife into the large end of the shrimp, cutting in about 3/4 of the way to the back, then cutting to the tail. Be careful not to cut through the shrimp. Rinse the shrimp clean & set aside. Medium chop fresh basil & oregano by hand, measure and set aside. Dice the tomatoes into a medium dice about 1/4 inch, measure and set aside. Crumble feta cheese, measure and set aside. Prepare pasta according to package directions, drain, and keep warm. On a stovetop, in a large saucepan, heat the Primavera Sauce, basil, oregano, and shrimp for 3-4 minutes. Add feta cheese and tomatoes and cook until shrimp is pink in color. Add mixture to cooked pasta and fold, mixing well. Divide evenly on four plates top with chopped parsley and serve.

HINTS

Δ 1 In the restaurant, we use what are called 21 x 25 Shrimp. This means 21-25 shrimp to the pound, and they are jumbo shrimp. Another common size is 15 x 20 a bit larger, and as good for this recipe. You may find IQF (individually Quick Frozen) shrimp with the shell on. Do not buy cooked shrimp. If you find E-Z Peel shrimp, buy them - they have been cleaned and the shell will pull off easily, and are worth the extra cost. Δ 2 For the most professional looking dish, carefully leave tail on the shrimp when removing from the shell.

VARIATIONS

◊ Any style pasta noodle works with this recipe.

SUGGESTED WINES

Dry, light or medium white:
Good Harbor Chardonnay

OR

Dry, sparkling:
L. Mawby Cremant

SUGGESTED DINNER MENU

Wild Mushroom Cheesecake (pg 62)

Salad Leelanau (pg 77)

Greek Shrimp

Lemon Poppyseed Biscuits & Fresh Strawberries (pg 170)

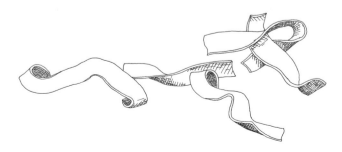

PASTA PRIMAVERA ♣

Cooks Notes

YIELD   4 SERVINGS

INGREDIENTS

1 Cup	Primavera Sauce (pg 49)
1 Lb	Pasta
4	Mushrooms - thinly sliced
2 Cups	Broccoli Flowerets
$^1/_2$ Cup	Baby Carrots
1 Cup	Snap Peas
1 Cup	Zucchini - julienne sliced
2 Tbls	Fresh Parsley - chopped

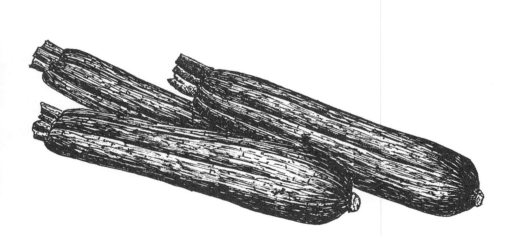

PREPARATION

Chop parsley and set aside. Prepare Primavera Sauce per recipe and set aside. Prepare pasta according to package directions, drain, and keep warm. Prepare sets by slicing mushrooms and zucchini. In a large sauté pan, over high heat add Primavera Sauce. Add mushrooms, broccoli, carrots, snap peas and zucchini. Cook for 3 minutes. Remove from heat and add mixture to cooked pasta and fold, mixing well. Divide evenly on four plates top with chopped parsley and serve.

VARIATIONS

◊ Any style pasta noodle works with this recipe.

SUGGESTED WINES

Dry, light to medium white:
Good Harbor Fishtown

OR

Semi-dry, light or medium White:
Good Harbor Trillium

SUGGESTED DINNER MENU

Garlic Shrimp (pg 69)

Salad Leelanau (pg 77)

Pasta Primavera

Hot Brandie Peaches
(pg 172)

MONKFISH & SCALLOP PRIMAVERA

YIELD	6 SERVINGS

INGREDIENTS

3 Cups	Primavera Sauce (pg 49)
12 oz	Monkfish Δ1 ◊2
2 Cups	Pasta ◊1
3/4 Cup	Mushrooms - sliced
6 oz	Sea Scallops - halved
12 oz	Shrimp Δ2
36	Mussels
3 Tbls	Fresh Parsley - chopped

PREPARATION

Chop parsley and set aside. Prepare the Primavera Sauce per recipe. Slice mushrooms. Cut Monkfish into 1-inch portions. Cut scallops in half. Remove shrimp from the shell Δ2 and lay on side. Butterfly the shrimp by carefully inserting sharp knife into the large end of the shrimp, cutting in about 3/4 of the way to the back, then cutting to the tail. Be careful not to cut through the shrimp. Rinse the shrimp clean & set aside Δ3. Clean and de-beard mussels. Prepare pasta according to package directions, drain, and keep warm. In a large sauté pan, heat Primavera Sauce and mushrooms. Add Monkfish, scallops, shrimps and mussels. Cook on low heat for 2 minutes. Be sure to stir all seafood frequently so it is evenly cooked. Cover the pan and cook an additional 3 minutes. This will allow the mussels to open. In a large bowl, combine pasta, seafood mixture (hold back mussels) and toss. Divide equally into pasta bowls, garnish with 6 mussels per serving and sprinkle with chopped parsley.

HINTS

Δ1 The importance of quality fish cannot be over emphasized. The difference between a superb fish dinner and an ordinary dinner begins with the quality of the fish. Δ2 In the restaurant, we use what are called 21 x 25 Shrimp. This means 21-25 shrimp to the pound, and they are jumbo shrimp. Another common size is 15 x 20 a bit larger, and as good for this recipe. You may find IQF (individually Quick Frozen) shrimp with the shell on. Do not buy cooked shrimp. If you find E-Z Peel shrimps, buy them - they have been cleaned and the shell will pull off easily, and are worth the extra cost. Δ3 For the most professional looking dish, carefully leave tail on the shrimp when removing from the shell.

VARIATIONS

◊1 Any style pasta noodle works with this recipe. ◊2 If Monkfish is not available several fresh lake and ocean fish are excellent with this breading including Whitefish, Lake Trout, Perch, Schrod, Salmon and many others.

SUGGESTED WINES

Dry, light or medium white:
Good Harbor Chardonnay

OR

Dry, sparkling:
L. Mawby Cremant

SUGGESTED DINNER MENU

Garlic Shrimp (pg 69)

Salad Leelanau (pg 77)

Monkfish & Scallop Primavera

Turtle Brownie (pg 174)

MUSHROOM MADNESS

Cooks Notes

YIELD   4 SERVINGS

INGREDIENTS

4 Cups	Pasta ◊1
2 Cups	Heavy Cream
2 Cups	Half & Half
2 Cups	Water
1/2 Cup	Porcini Mushrooms - dried, sliced ◊2
1/2 Cup	Morel Mushrooms - dried, sliced ◊2
1/2 Cup	Shittaki Mushrooms - sliced ◊2
1/2 Cup	Parmesan Cheese - grated
2 Tbls	Black Peppercorns - crushed
4 Tbls	Fresh Parsley - chopped

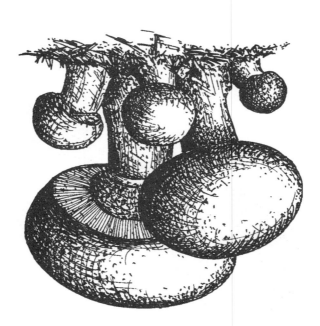

PREPARATION

Chop parsley and set aside. In a saucepan, bring water to a boil and cook Porcini and Morels for 20 minutes. Drain, slice and set aside. Prepare pasta according to package directions. Drain and keep warm. In a large sauté pan, combine heavy cream, Half & Half and sliced mushrooms. Boil for about 2 minutes, stirring to prevent scorching. Add Parmesan cheese and crushed peppercorns stirring well. Allow sauce to cook to thicken for 1 minute. To serve, divide pasta evenly on 4 dinner plates. Top with equal amounts of sauce and sprinkle with chopped parsley.

VARIATIONS

◊1 Any style pasta noodle. ◊2 Any mushroom works with this recipe.

SUGGESTED WINES

Dry, medium white:
Good Harbor Chardonnay

OR

Dry, light to medium red:
Boskydel DeChaunac

SUGGESTED DINNER MENU

Boursin Cheese (pg 66)

Salad Leelanau (pg 77)

Mushroom Madness

Strawwberries Cream Anglaise (pg 167)

SPANISH DELIGHT ♣

YIELD   4 SERVINGS

INGREDIENTS

1¹/₂ Cup	Primavera Oil (pg 49)
1 Cup	Sun Dried Tomatoes - julienne, sliced Δ1
2 Cup	Artichoke Hearts - chopped
1 Cup	Pine Nuts - toasted
2 Cup	Feta Cheese - crumbled
1 Cup	Kalamata Olives - sliced lengthwise ◊1
2 Cup	Pasta ◊2
2 Tbls	Fresh Parsley - chopped

Cooks Notes

PREPARATION
Chop parsley and set aside. Prepare the Primavera Sauce per recipe. Prepare pasta according to package directions, drain, and keep warm. Medium-chop the sun dried tomatoes and artichoke hearts and set aside. Heat the Primavera Sauce and add the sun-dried tomatoes, artichoke hearts, olives and toasted pine nuts. Heat mixture for 3-4 minutes, add the feta cheese, and add mixture to cooked pasta and fold, mixing well. Divide evenly on four plates top with chopped parsley and serve.

HINTS
Δ If the tomatoes are packed dry, steam or poach to soften before use; if packed in oil, drain and slice.

VARIATIONS
◊1 Ripe black olives may be substituted. ◊2 Any style pasta noodle works with this recipe.

SUGGESTED WINES

Dry, medium white:
Good Harbor Chardonnay

OR

Dry, light to medium red:
Boskydel DeChaunac

SUGGESTED DINNER MENU

Crab & Avocado
Quesadilla (pg 68)

Salad Leelanau (pg 77)

Spanish Delight

Chocolate Mousse
Cake (pg 180)

PRIME RIB STROGANOFF ♣

SUGGESTED WINES

Dry, medium to heavy white:
L. Mawby Vignoles

OR

Dry, light to medium red:
Good Harbor Coastal Red

SUGGESTED DINNER MENU

Stuffed Potabella Mushroom Caps (pg 59)

Salad Leelanau (pg 77)

Prime Rib Stroganoff

Chocolate Mousse Cake (pg 180)

YIELD   4 SERVINGS

INGREDIENTS

4 Cups	Swiss Onion Soup (pg 194)
3 Cups	Prime Rib - cubed ◊1
4 Cups	Pasta ◊2
2 Tbls	Fresh Parsley - chopped

PREPARATION

Chop parsley and set aside. Prepare pasta according to package directions, drain, and keep warm. In a large sauté pan, combine Swiss Onion Soup and prime rib. Heat to a boil. Cook the mixture for about 3 minutes at a boil, stirring to prevent scorching. To serve, divide pasta evenly on 4 dinner plates, top with equal amounts of sauce, and sprinkle with chopped parsley.

VARIATIONS

◊1 At the Inn we slow roast our prime for 12 hours, then cut into 1-inch cubes for the stroganoff. Other high quality meats such as strip loin or filet, will work fine. If using the strip loin or filet, season the meat to your liking, char grill, remove all fat, and cut into 1-inch cubes. ◊2 Any style pasta noodle works with this recipe.

LAKE & OCEAN FISH AND OTHER OCEAN FAVORITES

"Well, Mr. Baldwin, *this* is a pretty
kettle of fish!"

-Queen Mary

DITTO'S TUNA SURPRISE

Cooks Notes

YIELD   LOTS

INGREDIENTS

$^1/_2$ Cup	Whole Wheat Flour
1 Cup	Flour
1 Pkg	Unflavored Gelatin
1 Pkg	Dry Yeast
1 Cup	Water - warm
$^1/_2$ Cup	Oil
1	Egg
1 Can	Tuna
$^1/_4$ Cup	Water

PREPARATION

Preheat oven to 325 degrees. In a mixing bowl, combine yeast and warm water and mix until yeast is dissolved. In another mixing bowl, combine all dry ingredients and mix. Add water, oil, egg, drained tuna, and yeast mixture. Mix well by hand. On a greased sheet pan, evenly space 1 Tbl size balls and bake for 25 minutes. Remove from oven and cool completely before serving.

HINTS

If you have not figured it out by the name of this recipe, this is a treat for your four legged family members. However, as you can see by the ingredients, all family members may enjoy.

VARIATIONS

◊ Ditto sometimes preferred canned salmon in place of tuna.

LEMON LEEK STUFFED SALMON

YIELD	6 SERVINGS

INGREDIENTS

6 - 8oz	Salmon Fillets Δ
$^1/_4$ Cup	Onions - finely diced
$^1/_4$ Cup	Celery - finely diced
1	Leek - $^1/_4$ inch chopped
1 $^1/_4$ Cup	Bread Crumbs
$^1/_2$ Cup	Butter - clarified
2 Tbls	Chives - fresh, chopped
1 Tbl	White Wine
1 Tbl	Fresh Lemon Juice
Titch	Salt
Titch	White Pepper - ground
1	Egg
3	Lemons
4 Cups	Lemon Butter Sauce (Pg 196)
$^1/_2$ Cup	Chives - fresh, chopped

PREPARATION

Preheat oven to 350 degrees. Clarifying Butter: In a medium sauté pan, melt butter allowing solids to settle. Carefully pour off liquid - this is clarified butter. Plan on losing 25% of beginning volume. Prepare Lemon Butter Sauce per recipe then add $^1/_2$ cup chopped chives, mix well and set aside. Prepare sets by chopping onions and celery and set aside. Slice leeks $^1/_4$ inch thick (white parts only) and set aside. Take the green stems of the leek and cut them julienne style and set aside. In a medium sauté pan, over medium heat, add clarified butter. Heat, then add onions, celery and leeks. Cook for 3 minutes, add bread crumbs, 1 Tbl chives, wine, lemon juice, salt, pepper and egg. Mix well, remove from heat and chill. Prepare salmon fillets by inserting a sharp knife at the top end of the fillet and slitting towards the bottom creating a pocket lengthwise. Evenly divide chilled stuffing into 6 portions and press the stuffing into the slit, leaving about $1/2$ inch exposed outside the slit. On a sheet pan lay 6 stuffed salmon fillets and bake for 15 minutes. Remove from oven placing each fillet on the center of a plate. Top with lemon butter chive sauce. Garnish with julienne sliced leeks and serve.

VARIATIONS
Δ The importance of quality fish cannot be over emphasized. The difference between a superb fish dinner and an ordinary dinner begins with the quality of the fish. This stuffing works well with any medium to full flavored fresh water or ocean fillet.

SUGGESTED WINES

Dry, light or medium white:
Good Harbor Chardonnay

OR

Semi-dry, light or medium White:
Good Harbor Trillium

SUGGESTED DINNER MENU

Smoked Salmon with Red Radish Dill Sauce (pg 70)

Salad Leelanau (pg 77)

Lemon Leek Stuffed Salmon

Apple Mound (pg 186)

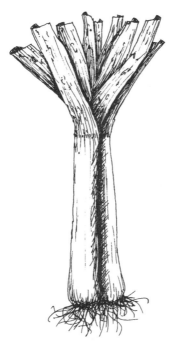

Salmon EnCroute

YIELD   6 SERVINGS

INGREDIENTS

$^1/_4$ Cup	Butter
6 - 8 oz.	Salmon Fillets - Skinned ◊ Δ1
1 Cup	Spinach - drained, chopped Δ2
4 Tbls	Shallots - minced
$^1/_2$ Cup	Mushrooms - chopped
4 Tbls	Basil - fresh, chopped
$1^1/_4$ Cup	White Wine
$^1/_2$ Cup	Parmesan Cheese - grated
4 Tbls	Butter
2 Tbls	Flour
$^3/_4$ Cup	Half and Half
3 Sheets	Puff Pastry Δ3
1	Egg
3 Tbl	Water
$^1/_2$ Cup	Lemon Butter Sauce (pg 196)
1	Whole Lemon

PREPARATION

Squeeze spinach dry Δ2. Chop and set aside. Prepare
sets by mincing shallots, chopping mushrooms and setting aside. Δ3 Remove puff pastry from freezer and thaw
completely. Δ4 Preheat convection oven to 350 degrees.
With a sharp knife carefully remove the skin from the
bottom of the salmon fillet. In a sauce pan, heat white
wine add shallots, mushroom, $1^1/_4$ cup butter, basil and
simmer for 15 minutes. In a double boiler, heat the
cream. In a sauté pan melt 2oz butter, add flour, cooking for 2 minutes. Add heated cream and cook until
smooth. Remove from heat. Add Parmesan cheese and
spinach. Mix completely and set aside. Cut one sheet of
puff pastry in half. Place one salmon fillet in the center
in one half of the puff pastry. Spread $^1/_6$ of the spinach
mixture on top of the fish. Place the second half of the
pastry on the fish and seal by pressing your fingertips

along the perimeter of the fish pinching it closed. With a knife remove the remaining pastry and discard. In a mixing bowl, beat egg in water and brush this mixture on the top of the finished prepped product. Bake for 20 minutes. Carefully slice lemon into 6 slices. Remove EnCroute and place on plate. Top with Lemon Butter Sauce and garnish with fresh basil and lemon slice.

HINTS

Δ1 The importance of quality fish cannot be over emphasized. The difference between a superb fish dinner and a ordinary dinner begins with the quality of the fish. Δ2 It is important that the spinach be as dry as possible, as excessive moisture results in a stuffing that will not hold together. To dry spinach, place the spinach in the center of a kitchen towel, bring up the sides and twist the cloth to squeeze out excess moisture. Δ3 This puff pastry may be found at many food stores in the freezer section. One box contains two sheets, each 14 x 11 inches. Δ4 This dish is best when cooked in a convection oven. If a convection oven is not available, cook in a preheated conventional oven at 400 degrees for 25 minutes. To achieve a golden brown color it may be necessary to broil for 1-2 minutes.

VARIATIONS

◊ This recipe works well with any medium or full flavor fish i.e. Whitefish, Cape Bluefish, Walleye.

SUGGESTED WINES

Dry, medium or heavey white:
L. Mawby Vignole

OR

Semi-dry, light or medium White:
Boskydel Soleil Blanc

SUGGESTED DINNER MENU

Stuffed Portabella Mushroom Caps (pg 59)

Southern Spinach Salad (pg 77)

Salmon EnCroute

Bailey's Irish Cream Chocolate Paté (pg 184)

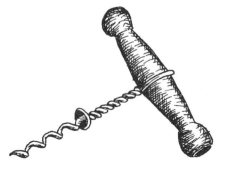

SALMON ENPAPILLOTE

YIELD   4 SERVINGS

INGREDIENTS

4 - 8 oz	Salmon Fillets Δ1 ◊
4 oz	Butter
4 tsp	Ginger - fresh, grated
2	Oranges
2	Lemons
2	Green Onions - chopped
2 Sheets	Baker Sheet Paper Δ2
2 Tbls	Fresh Parsley - chopped

PREPARATION

Chop parsley and set aside. Prepare sets by skinning salmon, chopping onion, grating the ginger, and grating zest from lemon and oranges. Squeeze the juice from 1 lemon and 1 orange and set aside. Cut the remaining lemon and orange into 4 equal slices each and set aside. Preheat oven to 350 degrees. Δ2 Prepare parchment by cutting each sheet in half lengthwise (Fig. 1), then fold each piece in half to crease, then lay open (Fig.2). Place each fillet on a piece of paper next to the crease (Fig.3). Top and evenly divide butter, ginger, oranges, lemons and green onions, chopped parsley on the top of each fillet. Fold sheet paper over fillet, folding the edges tightly together (Fig.4), making certain the parchment is sealed. Place parchments on a sheet pan and bake for 18 minutes. Remove from oven. Place each parchment on a separate dinner plate and bring to the table still sealed. At the table, cut the folded edge of the parchment (be careful of steam), pull parchment away from fillet and serve.

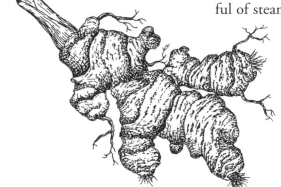

HINTS

Δ1 The importance of quality fish cannot be over emphasized. The difference between a superb fish dinner and a ordinary dinner begins with the quality of the fish.
Δ2 Baker's sheet paper can be found at most food stores: 16 ½ inch x 24 ½ inch is the standard size that we use at the Inn.

VARIATIONS

◊ If Salmon is not available several fresh lake and ocean fish are excellent, including Whitefish, Lake Trout, Perch, Schrod, Monkfish and many others.

SUGGESTED WINES

Dry, medium or heavey white:
Leelanau Chardonnay

OR

Dry medium rose:
Boskydel Rose de Chaunac

SUGGESTED DINNER MENU

Garlic Shrimp (pg 69)

Tortellini Salad (pg 76)

Salmon EnPapillote

Turtle Brownie (pg 174)

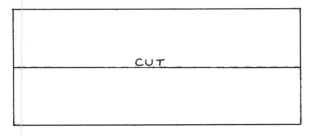

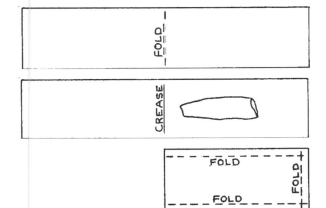

Cooks Notes

MARINATED BABY HALIBUT WITH CANTALOUPE SALSA ♣

YIELD	6 SERVINGS

INGREDIENTS

2	Garlic Cloves - halved
1/4 tsp	White Pepper - ground
2 Tbls	Sugar
1/3 Cup	Soy Sauce
6 Tbls	Canola Oil
3	Green Onions - finely chopped
1 Tbl	Sesame Seed
6 - 8 oz	Halibut Steaks - ◊ Δ1
3 Cups	Cantaloupe Salsa (pg 35)

PREPARATION

Prepare Cantaloupe Salsa per recipe and refrigerate. Δ2 Prepare sets by cutting garlic cloves in half and fine chopping green onions. In a mixing bowl, add all ingredients. Mix well, cover and refrigerate at least 12 hours. Δ3 Remove from refrigeration and after placing the Halibut steaks in a casserole dish cover steaks with marinade. Refrigerate for 3 hours turning steaks every 30 minutes. At the Inn we char grill the Halibut steaks about 3 1/2 minutes per side to achieve a medium rare. If a char grill is not available, bake the Halibut in an oven at 350 degrees for 10 minutes. After cooking place Halibut in the center of a plate and top with 1/4 cup Cantaloupe Salsa and serve.

HINTS

Δ1 The importance of quality fish cannot be over emphasized. The difference between a superb fish dinner and an ordinary dinner begins with the quality of the fish. Δ2 Salsa may be stored under refrigeration for up to 3 days. Δ3. Marinade once used should be discarded. Unused marinade may be stored refrigerated for up to 7 days.

VARIATIONS

◊ This marinade works well with Swordfish, Tuna, Mako Shark and Salmon.

SUGGESTED WINES

Dry, light or medium white:
Good Harbor Chardonnay

OR

Dry, sparkling:
L. Mawby Cremant

SUGGESTED DINNER MENU

Crab Cakes (pg 65)

Salad Leelanau (pg 77)

Marinated Baby Halibut with Cantaloupe Salsa

Hot BrandiedPeaches (pg 172)

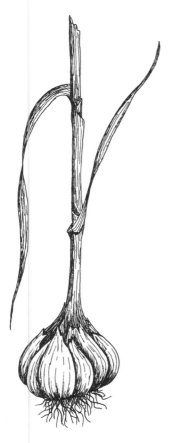

STUFFED LOUP deMER (WOLFISH) WITH SALMON MOUSSE ♣

YIELD	4 SERVINGS

INGREDIENTS

4 - 8 oz	Wolfish Fillets ◊ Δ

Mousse

6 oz	Salmon - fresh
3 oz	Scallops
2 oz	Cream Cheese
2 Tbls	Heavy Whipping Cream
2 Tbls	Dill - fresh
2 Tbls	Bread Crumbs
1/4 tsp	Black Pepper
1/4 tsp	Salt
8 oz	Lemon Butter Sauce (pg 196)
2 Tbls	Fresh Parsley - chopped

PREPARATION

Chop parsley and set aside. Prepare Lemon Butter Sauce per recipe and set aside. Prepare sets by skinning salmon and dicing. In a food processor, combine all ingredients and puree. Place mousse in a pastry bag and set aside. Preheat oven to 350 degrees. Curl fish into a round tube shape, secure with a toothpick and set on a greased sheet pan. Using the pastry bag, evenly divide the mousse by piping into the center of the curled fish. Bake for 20 minutes. Remove from oven, place on a serving plate, top with Lemon Butter Sauce and chopped parsley. Ready to serve.

HINTS

Δ The importance of quality fish cannot be over empha-sized. The difference between a superb fish dinner and an ordinary dinner begins with the quality of the fish. To achieve fuller flavor, leave steaks in marinade for a longer period of time.

VARIATIONS

◊ If Wolfish is not available several fresh lake and ocean fish are excellent, including Whitefish, Lake Trout, Perch, Salmon, Schrod, Monkfish and many others.

SUGGESTED WINES

Dry, medium or heavy white:
Good Harbor Pinot Gris

OR

Semi-dry, light or medium white:
Leelanau Winter White

SUGGESTED DINNER MENU

Boursin Cheese (pg 66)

Southern Spinach Salad (pg 74)

Stuffed Loup deMer with Salmon Mousse

Praline Ice Cream Pie (pg 176)

BROILED SCALLOPS

Cooks Notes

YIELD   4 SERVINGS

INGREDIENTS

24 oz	Sea Scallops Δ1
1 Cup	Dry Batter Mix (Drakes)
1 Tbl	Paprika
2 tsps	Salt
4 oz	Garlic Butter Sauce (Pg 197)
1	Whole Lemon

PREPARATION

Season Scallops with salt. In a mixing bowl, combine scallops and batter mix. Thoroughly dust scallops; Δ2 remove scallops from excess batter mix and place on a broiler pan. Top with paprika and place under broiler 3-4 minutes, or until golden brown. Quarter lemon. Remove from broiler and divide evenly and top with Garlic Butter Sauce. Garnish with lemon quarter and serve.

HINTS

Δ The importance of quality fish cannot be over empha-sized. The difference between a superb fish dinner and an ordinary dinner begins with the quality of the fish.
Δ2 It is important that the scallops are well dusted, but that excess batter mix is removed.

VARIATIONS

Makes a great appetizer and can be enhanced by marinat-ing scallops in some dry sherry.

SUGGESTED WINES

Dry, light to medium white:
Good Harbor Fishtown

OR

Semi-dry, light or medium White:
Good Harbor Trillium

SUGGESTED DINNER MENU

Asiago cheese Crostini (pg 67)

Salad Leelanau (pg 77)

Broiled Scallops

Chocolate Cheesecake (pg 182)

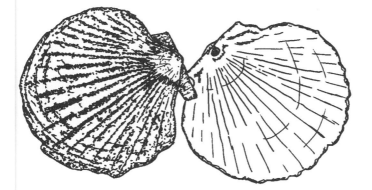

PAN FRIED BABY HALIBUT ALMONDINE

YIELD   4 SERVINGS

INGREDIENTS

4 - 8 oz	Halibut Steaks Δ1 ◊
1 Cup	Almondine Breading (pg. 198)
2	Eggs
3/4 Cup	Water
1/2 Cup	Flour
1/2 Cup	Butter
1/2 Cup	Lemon Butter Sauce (pg 196)
2 Tbls	Fresh Parsley - chopped

PREPARATION

Chop Parsley and set aside. Prepping the fish: With Halibut Fillets, there are no bones to be concerned with. However, you should remove the skin from the fillet or steak. In a small mixing bowl, mix egg and water together to make an egg wash. Place flour in a shallow pan and arrange fish to the left of the flour, egg wash to the right. Place Almondine Breading in a shallow pan to the right of the egg wash. Δ2 Prepare fish by dredging through flour, dusting off extra flour, then dipping in egg wash and placing in breading, coating both sides of fish with breading. As each fillet is breaded, place in the refrigerator to hold prior to cooking. Preheat sauté pan, add butter, melt and get hot without burning. Place fish in hot butter and cook on each side until golden brown, about three minutes each side. To serve, place each fillet or steak on a dinner plate and top each with 2 Tbls Lemon Butter Sauce and sprinkle with chopped parsley.

HINTS

Δ1 The importance of quality fish cannot be over emphasized. The difference between a superb fish dinner and an ordinary dinner begins with the quality of the fish. Δ2 When breading the fillet or steak use a two handed method. One hand remains dry and the other hand is used to dip the fish into the egg wash. By doing this you will not end up with a pound of breading stuck to your fingers.

VARIATIONS

◊ If Halibut is not available several fresh lake and ocean fish are excellent, including Whitefish, Lake Trout, Pickerel, Perch, Salmon, Schrod, Monkfish and many others.

SUGGESTED WINES

Dry, medium or heavy white:
Good Harbor Pinot Gris

OR

Semi-dry, light or medium White:
Good Harbor Trillium

SUGGESTED DINNER MENU

Wild Mushroom Cheesecake (pg 62)

Salad Leelanau (pg 77)

Pan Fried Halibut Almondine

Chocolate Mousse Cake (pg 180)

PECAN TUNA ♣

YIELD   4 SERVINGS

INGREDIENTS

4 - 8oz	Yellowfin Tuna Steaks ◊1
2 oz	Pecans - finely chopped
1 Cup	Bread Crumbs
Titch	Salt
Titch	White Pepper - ground
2	Eggs
3/4 Cup	Water
1/2 Cup	Flour
1/2 Cup	Butter - clarified
1 Cup	Mustard Sauce (pg 40)
2 Tbl	Fresh Parsley - chopped

PREPARATION

Chop parsley and set aside. Prepare Mustard Sauce per recipe and keep warm. Clarifying Butter: In a medium saucepan, melt butter allowing solids to settle. Carefully pour off liquid - this is clarified butter. Plan on losing 25% of beginning volume. Prepare pecans by chopping fine. In a small mixing bowl, mix egg and water together to make an egg wash. Place flour in a shallow pan and arrange fish to the left of the flour, egg wash to the right. Place pecan mixture in a shallow pan to the right of the egg wash. Δ2 Prepare fish by dredging through flour, dusting off extra flour, then dipping in egg wash and placing in breading and coating both sides of fish with breading. As each steak is breaded, place in the refrigerator to hold prior to cooking. Preheat sauté pan, add butter, melt and get hot without burning. Place fish in hot butter and cook on each side, about 3 minutes a side. To serve, place each steak on a dinner plate and top with 2 Tbls of Mustard Sauce and sprinkle with chopped parsley.

HINTS

Δ1 The importance of quality fish cannot be over emphasized. The difference between a superb fish dinner and an ordinary dinner begins with the quality of the fish. Δ2 When breading the fillet or steak use a two handed method. One hand remains dry and the other hand is used to dip the fish into the egg wash. By doing this you will not up end with a pound of breading stuck to your fingers.

VARIATIONS

◊ If Tuna is not available several fresh lake and ocean fish are excellent with this breading including Whitefish, Lake Trout, Pickerel, Perch, Salmon, Schrod, Monkfish and many others.

SUGGESTED WINES

Dry, medium to heavy white:
L. Mawby Vignoles

OR

Dry, light to medium red:
Good Harbor Coastal Red

SUGGESTED DINNER MENU

Crab & Avacado Quesadilla (pg 68)

Salad Leelanau (pg 77)

Pecan Tuna

White Chocolate Cake & Raspberry Sauce (pg 178)

CORN MEAL CRUSTED WOLFISH ♣

YIELD   6 SERVINGS

INGREDIENTS

Corn Meal Crust
1 Cup	Milk
1	Egg
1¹/2 Cups	Corn Meal
2 tsps	Salt
1 tsp	Black Pepper - ground
¹/2 tsp	Cayenne Pepper
5 - 8 oz	Wolfish Fillets Δ1 ◊1
¹/2 Cup	Butter - clarified
2¹/2 Cups	Moulin Rouge Sauce (pg 55) ◊2
2 Tbl	Fresh Parsley - chopped

PREPARATION

Chop parsely and set aside. Clarifying Butter: In a medium saucepan, melt butter, allowing solids to settle. Carefully pour off liquid - this is clarified butter. Plan on losing 25% of beginning volume. Prepping the fish: In a small mixing bowl, mix milk and egg together to make an egg wash. In another mixing bowl, combine corn meal, salt, black pepper and cayenne pepper and mix well. Place this breading in a shallow pan to the right of the egg wash. Δ2 Prepare fish by dredging through the egg wash and place in breading coating both sides. As each fillet is breaded, place in the refrigerator to hold prior to cooking. Preheat sauté pan, add butter, and get hot without burning. Place fish in hot butter and cook on each side until golden brown, about 3 minutes a side. To serve, place fillet on a dinner plate and top with Moulin Rouge Sauce and sprinkle with chopped parsley.

Hints

Δ1 The importance of quality fish cannot be over emphasized. The difference between a superb fish dinner and an ordinary dinner begins with the quality of the fish. Δ2 When breading the fillet or steak use a two handed method. One hand remains dry and the other hand is used to dip the fish into the egg wash. By doing this you will not end up with a pound of breading stuck to your fingers.

Variations

◊1 If Wolfish is not available several fresh lake and ocean fish are excellent with this breading, including Whitefish, Lake Trout, Pickerel, Perch, Salmon, Schrod, Monkfish and many others. ◊2 Another compliment sauce would be the Mustard Sauce (pg 40).

Suggested Wines

Dry, medium to heavy white:
Boskydel Vignoles

Or

Semi-dry, light to medium red:
Good Harbor Harbor Red

Suggested Dinner Menu

Mini Whitefish Neptune (pg 63)

Salad Leelanau (pg 77)

Cornmeal Crusted Wolfish

Bread Pudding with Dried Cherries & White Chocolate Sauce (pg 168)

Char Grilled Tuna with Shrimp Sauce ♣

YIELD   4 SERVINGS

INGREDIENTS

4 - 8oz	Tuna Steaks Δ1 ◊
1/4 Cup	Canola Oil
1/2 Cup	Red Wine Shrimp Sauce (pg 44)
2 Tbls	Fresh Parsley - chopped

PREPARATION

Chop parsley and set aside. Cooking will be done on an open flame char grill preheated so that the rack is HOT. Doing this will seer the steak so that the meat should not stick to the rack. Brush both sides of the steak with oil and lay on the grill rack. Cook uncovered Δ2, grill 2 minutes then rotate steak 90 degrees and cook another 2 minutes. This procedure produces a nice 'checkerboard' of grill lines on the steak. After 8 minutes total cooking time Δ3, remove the fish from the grill and place each steak on a dinner plate. Top each with 2 Tbls of Red Wine Shrimp Sauce. Sprinkle with chopped parsley and serve.

HINTS

Δ1 The importance of quality fish can not be over emphasized. The difference between a superb fish dinner and an ordinary dinner begins with the quality of the fish. Δ2 Cooking on a covered grill will shorten cooking times given. Δ3 Tuna is best cooked medium rare. This fish tends to be dry if overcooked. If your grill is cooking hot and the Tuna starts to get too dark reduce the cooking time.

VARIATIONS

◊ The char grilling procedure can be used with any steak cut fish; or with firm fillet fish such as, Sturgeon, Whitefish, or Halibut. Some fillets of fish like, Sole and Schrod are so tender that they break apart on the grill and should not be used. A rule of thumb is that if the fillet is solid and firm it should stand up to the grill.

SUGGESTED WINES

Dry, medium white:
Good Harbor Chardonnay

OR

Dry, light to medium red:
Boskydel DeChaunac

SUGGESTED DINNER MENU

Garlic Shrimp (pg 69)

Salad Leelanau (pg 77)

Char Grilled Tuna & Shrimp Sauce

Lemon Ice Cream White Chocolate Tartufo (pg 188)

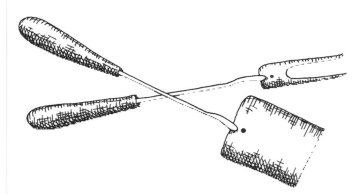

MUSTARD SWORDFISH

YIELD   4 SERVINGS

INGREDIENTS

4 - 8oz	Swordfish Steaks ◊1 Δ
1/4 Cup	White Wine
3 Cups	Water
3/4 Cup	Fresh Lemon Juice
2 Tbls	Fresh Parsley - chopped

Mustard Butter

6 Tbls	Butter - softened
3 Tbls	Fresh Lemon Juice
4 tsp	Country Dijon Mustard ◊2
3/4 tsp	Salt
1/2 tsp	Paprika

PREPARATION
Mustard Butter
Soften butter by allowing it to set at room temperature for at least 2 hours. In a mixing bowl, combine the butter, lemon juice, mustard, salt and paprika, mixing all ingredients together by hand.

Chop parsley and set aside. In a dish large enough for the 4 steaks to lay flat, mix lemon juice, wine and water. Lay steaks in the mixture and marinate for 10 minutes, then turn and marinate for 10 additional minutes. Remove steaks and place on a broiler pan. Generously coat one side of the steak with Mustard Butter, using 1 1/2 cups. Place under the broiler about 4 inches from the heat and cook for 6 minutes. Carefully turn steaks and generously coat the other side using 1 1/2 cups mustard butter returning to broiler for an additional 6 minutes. In a small saucepan, heat the remaining Mustard Butter. Remove steaks and place each on a dinner plate and pour melted Mustard Butter over. Sprinkle with chopped parsley and serve.

HINTS

Δ The importance of quality fish can not be over emphasized. The difference between a superb fish dinner and an ordinary dinner begins with the quality of the fish.

VARIATIONS

◊1 If Swordfish is not available several fresh lake and ocean fish are excellent with Mustard Butter, including Lake Trout, Salmon, Sturgeon, Tuna, Monkfish and many others. ◊2 For a little less 'bite', plain Dijon may be substituted for the country style Dijon.

SUGGESTED WINES

Dry, medium white:
Good Harbor Chardonnay

OR

Dry, light to medium red:
Boskydel DeChaunac

SUGGESTED DINNER MENU

Crab Cakes (pg 65)

Salad Leelanau (pg 77)

Mustard Swordfish

Caramel Dip & Fresh Fruit (pg 173)

JOHNNY'S FRIED SHRIMP ♣

YIELD   4 SERVINGS

INGREDIENTS

2 Cups	Batter Mix (Drakes)
1/2 tsp	Salt
2 Cups	Water
32	Jumbo Shrimp Δ1
1 Cup	Cocktail Sauce (pg 53)

This recipe is special to Linda, as it reminds her of a dish her dad would prepare for the family. We hope you enjoy it as much as they did.

PREPARATION

Remove shrimp from the shell Δ2 and lay on side. Butterfly the shrimp by carefully inserting sharp knife into the large end of the shrimp, cutting in about 3/4 of the way to the back, then cutting to the tail. Be careful not to cut through the shrimp. In a mixing bowl, combine batter mix and salt. Slowly add the water and mix until achieving a smooth consistency. In a large soup pot, place about 2-inch of peanut oil in the bottom and heat to about 375 degrees. Holding the butterflied shrimp by the tail, with your thumb and forefinger, dredge shrimp through the batter being careful not to get batter on the tail. Still holding its tail, carefully dredge the shrimp back and forth in the hot oil. It is important to 'blanch' the shrimp with the full 'butterfly' open so that both sides of the shrimp cook evenly. Once blanching has taken place, drop the shrimp in the pot and cook about 3 minutes or until golden brown.

Remove shrimp and set on paper towel to absorb grease. Now ready to serve.

Hints
Δ1 In the restaurant, we use what are called 21 x 25 Shrimp. This means 21-25 shrimp to the pound, and they are jumbo shrimp. Another common size is 15 x 20 a bit larger, and as good for this recipe. You may find IQF (individually Quick Frozen) shrimp with the shell on. Do not buy cooked shrimp. If you find E-Z Peel shrimps, buy them - they have been cleaned and the shell will pull off easily, and are worth the extra cost. Δ2 For the most professional looking dish, carefully leave tail on the shrimp when removing from the shell.

Suggested Wines

Dry, white:
L. Mawby Chardonnay

Or

Semi dry, light to medium white:
Good Harbor Fishtown

Suggested Dinner Menu

Wild Mushroom Cheesecake (pg 62)

Salad Leelanau (pg 77)

Johnny's Fried Shrimp

Lemon Poppyseed Biscuits & Fresh Strawberries (pg 170)

GRILLED SHRIMP ♣

YIELD	4 SERVINGS

INGREDIENTS

20	Jumbo-Jumbo Shrimp Δ1
5 Cups	Cherry Vinaigrette Dressing (pg 46)
8	Skewers
$^1/_2$ Cup	Cherry Pungent Fruit Sauce (pg 47)
2 Tbls	Fresh Parsley - chopped

PREPARATION

Chop parsley and set aside. Remove shrimp from the shell Δ2 and lay on side. Butterfly the shrimp by carefully inserting sharp knife into the large end of the shrimp, cutting in about $^3/_4$ of the way to the back, then cutting to the tail. Be careful not to cut through the shrimp. Rinse the shrimp clean & set aside. Dividing shrimp into 4 portions of 5 shrimp, using 2 skewers, pierce the head end of the shrimp with 1 skewer and the mid-section with the other. This stabilizes the product during grilling. Cooking will be done on an open flame char grill preheated so that the rack is HOT. Doing this will sear the steak so that the meat should not stick to the rack. Pour 4 $^1/_2$ cups Cherry Vinaigrette in a pan large enough to lay the 4 double skewers flat and marinade refrigerated for 1 hour. In a large sauté pan, heat the remaining Cherry Vinaigrette and get HOT. Char grill each double skewer for 2 minutes on each side. Remove the shrimp from skewers and sauté in the HOT vinaigrette for 5 minutes or until fully cooked. Be sure to turn shrimp frequently so that all areas cook evenly. Serve with Cherry Pungent Fruit Sauce and top with chopped parsley.

HINTS

Δ1 For this recipe we recommend the use of what are referred to as U-10 Shrimp. This signifies 10 shrimp to a pound. This is a very large shrimp and works best for grilling. You may find IQF (individually Quick Frozen) shrimp with the shell on. Do not buy cooked shrimp. If you find E-Z Peel shrimps, buy them - they have been cleaned and the shell will pull off easily, and are worth the extra cost. Δ2 For the most professional looking dish, carefully leave tail on the shrimp when removing from the shell.

SUGGESTED WINES

Semi dry, light to medium white:
Lelanau Winter White

OR

Dry, medium to heavy white:
Boskydel Soleil Blanc

SUGGESTED DINNER MENU

Boursin Cheese (pg 66)

Salad Leelanau (pg 77)

Grilled Shrimp

Fresh Strawberries Cream Anglaise (pg 167)

CAESAR SWORDFISH ♣

Cooks Notes

YIELD   4 SERVINGS

INGREDIENTS

4 -8 oz.	Swordfish Steaks Δ ◊
1 Cup	Caesar Fish Marinade (Pg. 43)
1/4 Lb	Caesar Butter (Pg. 41)
4 tsp	Parmesan Cheese - grated

PREPARATION

Prepare Caesar Marinade per recipe and set aside. Prepare Caesar Butter per recipe and set aside. Place Caesar Marinade in a casserole dish. Place 4 Swordfish steaks in the casserole dish and cover completely with marinade. Store in refrigerator for 3 hours turning steaks every 30 minutes. Cut Caesar Butter into four 1/4-inch slices. Preheat char grill. Place steaks on grill and cook 3 1/2 minutes per side. This cooking time will achieve a medium rare doneness. After turning steaks, and just prior to removal, place Caesar Butter in the center of the steak. Remove steak, place on platter, sprinkle with Parmesan cheese and serve.

HINTS

Δ The importance of quality fish cannot be over empha-sized. The difference between a superb fish dinner and a ordinary dinner begins with the quality of the fish. To achieve fuller flavor leave steaks in marinade for a longer period of time.

VARIATIONS

◊ This recipe works well with any steak cut fish, ie. Mako Shark, Tuna, & Halibut.

SUGGESTED WINES

Dry, medium to heavy white:
L. Mawby Pinot Gris

OR

Dry, light to medium red:
Boskydel DeChaunac

SUGGESTED DINNER MENU

Mini Whitefish Neptune (pg 63)

Salad Leelanau (pg 77)

Caesar Swordfish

Apple Mound (pg 186)

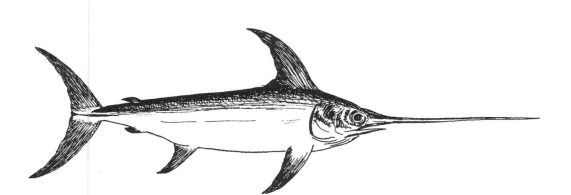

TEQUILA SWORDFISH ♣

YIELD   4 SERVINGS

INGREDIENTS

4 Cups	Olive Oil
1 Cup	White Wine
2 tsp	Red Pepper - crushed
1/2 Bunch	Cilantro - chopped
2	Lemons
2	Limes
2 tsp	Basil - fresh, chopped Δ1
2 Tbls	Thyme - fresh, chopped Δ1
2 Tbls	Dill - fresh, chopped Δ1
2 Tbls	Garlic Clove - minced Δ2 ◊
4 - 8 oz	Swordfish Steaks
1/4 Cup	Tequila
2 Tbls	Fresh Parsley - chopped
	Fresh Salsa (pg 39)

Preparation

Chop parsley and set aside. Prepare sets by chopping the cilantro, basil, thyme, dill, and squeezing the juice from the lemons & limes, and mincing garlic clove. In a large mixing bowl, combine the olive oil, white wine and your prepared sets, mixing completely. Dredge the Swordfish through this mixture covering completely. Refrigerate for 4 hours. After 4 hours pour Tequila on the Swordfish and marinate an additional hour. Preheat oven to 350 degrees. Place Swordfish on a sheet pan and bake for 12 minutes, or until they are firm. Place in the center of serving plate, top with Salsa and chopped parsley and serve.

Hints

Δ1 This is one dish that is best when using fresh herbs in place of dried. Δ2 The importance of quality fish cannot be over emphasized. The difference between a superb fish dinner and an ordinary dinner begins with the quality of the fish. To achieve fuller flavor, leave steaks in marinade for a longer period of time.

Variations

◊ If Swordfish is not available several fresh lake and ocean fish are excellent, including Whitefish, Lake Trout, Perch, Salmon, Schrod, Monkfish and many others.

Suggested Wines

Semi dry, medium white:
Good Harbor Riesling

Or

Dry, sparkling:
L.Mawby Blanc de Blancs

Suggested Dinner Menu

Garlic Shrimp (pg 69)

Salad Leelanau (pg 77)

Tequila Swordfish

Bailey's Irish Cream
Chocolate Paté (pg 184)

POULTRY & MEAT

"Kissing don't last; cookery do!"

-George Meredith

BUCCA'S BIRTHDAY FILET

Cooks Notes

YIELD   3 SERVINGS

INGREDIENTS

3 - 6oz   Beef Tenderloin

Marinade
3/4 Cup   Worcestershire Sauce
1/2 Cup   Fresh Lemon Juice
1 tsp   Garlic Puree
1 tsp   Paprika

PREPARATION
In a mixing bowl, combine ingredients for marinade and mix well. Marinate tenderloins for 6 hours being sure to turn often so that all sides are marinated. Remove from marinade and char grill to desired doneness (our kids prefer medium rare).

HINTS
If you have not figured it out by the name of this recipe, this is a treat for your four legged family members. However, as you can see by the ingredients, all family members may enjoy. Don't forget the birthday cake!

VARIATIONS
◊ Our kids prefer filet, however, strips or prime rib work also. I doubt that they will complain.

CHICKEN FLORENTINE ♧

YIELD   6 SERVINGS

INGREDIENTS

6 - 6 oz	Chicken Breasts - skinless and boneless ◊1
1 Tbl	Thyme - fresh, chopped
1 Tbl	Poultry Seasoning
1 Cup	Hot Bacon Sauce (pg 52)

Florentine Stuffing

2 Lbs	Spinach - frozen, chopped
3 1/2 Tbls	Canola Oil
4 1/2 Tbls	Butter
6 Slices	Bacon - diced
3/4 Cup	Onions - finely chopped
3/4 Cup	Dry White Wine ◊2
1 Tbl	Garlic Puree

PREPARATION

Florentine Stuffing

Squeeze spinach dry Δ. Chop and set aside. In a sauté pan, heat oil and butter over medium heat. Add bacon, cooking until crispy and well rendered. Add onions and sauté a couple of minutes. Add spinach, garlic and wine and simmer for 3 minutes. Cool and refrigerate for at least 1 hour before use.

With a tenderizing mallet pound chicken breasts flat using care to avoid tearing the meat. Preheat oven to 375 degrees. Lay each breast on a work surface with the inside of the breast facing up. Equally divide the Florentine stuffing by placing each portion in the center of the chicken breast. Fold tail end of breast up and over the stuffing. Fold each side of the breast up and over the stuffing, then invert the breast on to a baking pan. Sprinkle thyme and poultry seasoning on the top of the seasoned breasts. Bake for 20 minutes. Remove from oven and place each breast in the center of a serving plate, top with Hot Bacon Sauce and serve.

HINTS

Δ It is important that the spinach be as dry as possible, as excessive moisture results in stuffing that will not hold together. To dry spinach place the spinach in the center of a kitchen towel, bring up the sides, and twist the cloth to squeeze out excess moisture.

VARIATIONS

◊1 Chicken Breasts may be replaced with thick cut pork chops with Florentine stuffing placed in pockets cut into the chops. ◊2 The white wine may be replaced with sherry; or to make a heartier Florentine, with dry red wine.

USES

This stuffing is used in several fresh water and ocean fishes, shellfish and shrimp; also poultry and mushrooms.

SUGGESTED WINES

Semi-dry, light to medium white:
Good Harbor Fishtown

OR

Dry, medium red:
Leelanau Autumn Harvest

SUGGESTED DINNER MENU

Asiago Cheese Crotini (pg 67)

Salad Leelanau (pg 77)

Chicken Florentine

Turtle Brownie (pg 174)

Cornish 'Ginny' Hen

Cooks Notes

Yield   4 Servings

INGREDIENTS

4	Cornish Game Hens
Titch	Salt and Black Pepper
1/4 Cup	Canola Oil
12 oz	Demi Glaze Cream Sauce (pg 48)

Stuffing	
1/2 Cup	Butter
1/2 tsp	Garlic Puree
1/2 Cup	Celery - diced
1/2 Cup	Onion - diced
1 1/2 Cup	Shittaki Mushrooms - chopped
3 Cups	Herbal Bread - ground
1/2 Cup	Pecans - chopped
1 1/2 Cup	Water - hot
2 tsp	Chicken Bouillon
2 Tbls	Fresh Parsley - chopped

PREPARATION

Preheat oven to 350 degrees. Prepare herbal bread by grinding a flavorful herbed bread of your choice. Prepare sets by chopping and mincing as indicated. In a saucepan, melt the butter. Add garlic, celery, onions, and mushrooms then cook for about 4 minutes. Remove from heat. In a mixing bowl, combine herb bread, pecans and mushroom mixture, mixing well. Dissolve chicken bouillon in hot water and slowly add to breading until stuffing is moist. (You may not need it all.) Wash hens, pat dry and cut away any excess skin over the cavities. Salt and pepper hens. Brush hens with oil and stuff each hen with the pecan stuffing. Roast for 1 hour, 15 minutes. Prepare Demi Glaze Sauce according to recipe and keep warm. Remove the hens and after plating, top each hen with the Demi Glaze Sauce and chopped parsley.

SUGGESTED WINES

Semi-dry, medium white:
L. Mawby Sandpiper

OR

Dry, medium rose:
Boskydel Rose de Chaunac

SUGGESTED DINNER MENU

Crab Cakes (pg 65)

Salad Leelanau (pg 77)

Cornish 'Ginny' Hen

Chocolate Cheesecake (pg 182)

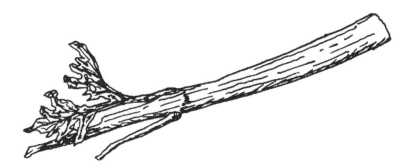

Rack of Lamb ♣

Cooks Notes

YIELD 4 SERVINGS

INGREDIENTS

4 - 12 oz	New Zealand Spring Rack
1/2 Cup	Olive Oil
1 Tbls	Basil - fresh, chopped
1 Tbls	Rosemary - fresh, chopped
1 tsp	Thyme - fresh, chopped
1	Garlic Clove - minced
1 tsp	Salt
1 tsp	Black Pepper - ground

PREPARATION

Prepare all sets by chopping or mincing where indicated. Remove fat cover and chine bone from rack and 'French' Δ cut the rib bones. In a mixing bowl, combine all ingredients, mix well and refrigerate for 1 hour. After 1 hour re-mix the marinade and generously cover each rack on all sides with the marinade and refrigerate for 24 hours. Preheat oven to 350 degrees. Cook lamb approximately 45 minutes or until the center reaches a center temperature of at least 140 degrees. Remove from oven and let sit for 5-10 minutes prior to serving. Enjoy.

HINTS

Δ 'French' cutting the bone is the process of stripping all fat from the tip of the bone $3/4$ of the way down the bone toward the meat.

VARIATIONS

◊ You can prepare the rack as described in this recipe, and slice between each rib, creating chops then char grill or broil to be served as a finger appetizer.

SUGGESTED WINES

Dry, medium red:
Good Harbor Coastal Red

OR

Dry, light to medium white:
Leelanau Winter White

SUGGESTED DINNER MENU

Crab & Avocado Quesadilla (pg 68)

Salad Leelanau (pg 77)

Rack of Lamb

Lemon Ice Cream White Chocolate Tartufo (pg 188)

VEAL PARMESAN ♣

YIELD   4 SERVINGS

INGREDIENTS

4 - 6 oz	Veal Cutlets
1	Egg
1 Cup	Water
1/4 Cup	Flour
1 Cup	Herbal Breading (pg 208)
1/2 Cup	Canola Oil
2 1/2 Cups	Provencale Sauce (pg 36) Δ1
8 oz Pkg	Mozzarella Cheese Slices
4 Tbls	Parmesan Cheese - grated

PREPARATION

Make an egg wash by vigorously beating egg and water together in a small bowl. Dust each cutlet in flour and dip in egg wash Δ2. Then dredge through the Herbal Breading making sure that all sides are covered. In a large sauté pan, add oil, heat sizzling hot without burning, add breaded veal and cook for 2 minutes. Turn and cook on other side for an additional 2 minutes. Set cutlets aside and cool Δ1. Preheat oven to 350 degrees. In a casserole large enough to lay the veal cutlets side by side, place 1 cup Provencale Sauce and spread evenly. Sprinkle 2 Tbls grated Parmesan cheese over the Provencale Sauce. Place veal cutlets in the casserole on top of sauce and top with remaining Provencale Sauce. Sprinkle remaining grated Parmesan over the top of sauce. Cut cheese slices in half and cover each veal cutlet with 2 pieces of cheese. Bake for 20 minutes and serve.

HINTS

Δ1 The correct preparation of this dish depends on using either all cool or all hot ingredients. If the Provencale Sauce that will be added is freshly made and hot do not cool cutlets, but assemble dish with warm veal and reduce baking time to 15 minutes. If you assemble dish with hot ingredients, do not cool before baking, as bacteria may grow in some parts of the casserole. If Provencale Sauce has been made ahead and is cool, follow preparation instructions. Δ2 When breading the veal use a two handed method. One hand remains dry, and the other hand is used to dip the veal into the egg wash. By doing this you will not end up with a pound of breading stuck to your fingers.

SUGGESTED WINES

Dry, medium to heavy white:
Good Harbor Vignoles

OR

Dry, medium red:
Leelanau Vis a Vis Red

SUGGESTED DINNER MENU

Smoked Salmon with Red Radish Dill Sauce (pg 70)

Salad Leelanau (pg 77)

Veal Parmesan

White Chocolate Cake & Raspberry Sauce (pg 178)

VEAL PICCATA

YIELD   4 SERVINGS

INGREDIENTS

4 - 6 oz	Veal Cutlets ◊
$^1/_8$ tsp	Salt
$^1/_4$ tsp	Black Pepper - ground
$^1/_4$ Cup	Flour
$^1/_2$ Cup	Butter
2 Tbls	Capers
3	Lemons - quartered
3 Tbls	Fresh Parsley - chopped

PREPARATION

Chop Parsley and set aside. With a tenderizing mallet pound veal cutlets flat using care to avoid tearing the meat. Season veal with salt and pepper, dredge through flour and remove any excess. In a sauté pan, melt $^1/4$ cup butter and heat to a foam, without burning. Place veal in sauté pan, and brown for 3 minutes each side for a total cooking time of 6 minutes. In a separate sauté pan, melt remaining butter and heat to a foam, without burning. Add capers and lemon quarters, squeezing lemons as they are added and sauté for 3 minutes. Then remove lemon quarters (and any seeds), and discard. Place veal in serving dish and top with caper butter sauce, then sprinkle with chopped parsley and serve.

VARIATIONS

◊ Chicken breast or pork tenderloin may be substituted for veal cutlet.

SUGGESTED WINES

Dry, sparkling:
L. Mawby Blanc de Blancs

OR

Dry, medium white:
Good Harbor Pinot Gris

SUGGESTED DINNER MENU

Wild Mushroom
Cheesecake (pg 62)

Salad Leelanau (pg 77)

Veal Piccata

Praline Ice Cream Pie
(pg 176)

AMY'S CHICKEN WELLINGTON ♣

YIELD	6 SERVINGS

INGREDIENTS

6 - 8oz	Chicken Breast - boneless
2 Cups	White Wine
1 Tbl	Basil - fresh, chopped
1 Tbl	Oregano - fresh, chopped
6 Sheets	Pepperidge Farm Puff Pastry Sheets Δ1
1	Egg
2 Tbls	Water
2 - 5.2oz	Boursin Cheese
2 1/2 Cups	Mushroom Veloute Sauce (pg 42)
2 Tbls	Fresh Parsley - chopped

PREPARATION

Chop parsley and set aside. Clean and trim chicken breasts. In a mixing bowl, combine white wine, basil, oregano and mix well. In a shallow glass dish, place chicken breasts and pour wine mixture on top to marinate. Refrigerate for 2 hours. Be sure to turn chicken breasts every half hour to insure all areas of the breasts are marinated. Prepare Mushroom Veloute Sauce per recipe and keep warm. Divide each Boursin into a third. Remove chicken breast from the marinade. In a sauté pan, place marinade, get hot and sauté chicken breasts over medium heat for 5 minutes. Remove and cool for about 20 minutes. Δ2 Preheat convection oven to 350 degrees. Cut puff pastry sheets in half. Using 6 halves, place each breast in the center. Top each chicken breast with a portion of Boursin Cheese. Place the remaining puff pastry on top of the chicken breast pinching the puff pastry sealed around the chicken. Cut the excess puff pastry away and discard. In a small mixing bowl, make an egg wash by mixing the egg and water together, then brush the top of the Wellington with egg wash. Bake for 20 minutes. Remove from oven and place each Wellington in the center of a serving plate and top with Mushroom Veloute Sauce, chopped parsley and serve.

HINTS

Δ1 This puff pastry can be found at many food stores in the freezer section. One box contains 2 sheets, each, 14 inches by 11 inches. Δ2 This dish is best when cooked in a convection oven. If a convection oven is not available, cook in preheated conventional oven at 375 degrees for 25 minutes. To achieve a golden brown color it may be necessary to broil for 1-2 minutes. Watch carefully so as not to burn.

SUGGESTED WINES

Dry, medium to heavy white:
Good Harbor Vignoles

OR

Light, medium red:
Leelanau Vis a Vis Red

SUGGESTED DINNER MENU

Whitefish Paté (pg)

Salad Leelanau (pg 77)

Amy's Chicken Wellington

Bread Pudding with Dried Cherries & White Chocolate Sauce (pg 168)

THANKSGIVING ACCOMPANIMENTS

"The best way to get the better of temptation
is just to yield to it."

-Clementina Stirling Graham

MOIRA'S TURKEY FEAST

YIELD	LOTS

INGREDIENTS

2 ¹/₂ Cups	Cooked Turkey ◊
3	Yams - cooked, chopped
1 ¹/₂ Tbls	Oil
1 ¹/₂ tsp	Bone Meal
¹/₄ Cup	Miniature Marshmallows

PREPARATION
Prepare sets by cutting turkey into bite size pieces and chopping yams. In a mixing bowl, combine all ingredients and mix well and serve.

HINTS
If you have not figured it out by the name of this recipe, this is a treat for your four legged family members. However, as you can see by the ingredients, all family members may enjoy.

VARIATIONS
◊ White or dark meat - our kids love them both. Depending on the individual whims of this family member feel free to substitute beef, chicken, or whatever they desire.

PUMPKIN BREAD

YIELD   2 LOAVES

Cooks Notes

INGREDIENTS

2 Cups	Sugar
1 Cup	Vegetable Oil
3	Eggs
16 oz Can	Pumpkin
3 Cups	Flour
1 tsp	Baking Soda
1/2 tsp	Salt
1/2 tsp	Baking Powder
1 tsp	Cinnamon - ground
1 tsp	Nutmeg - ground
1 Cup	Pecans - chopped
1 Cup	Raisins ◊

PREPARATION

Preheat oven to 325 degrees. In a large mixing bowl, whip together sugar and oil. Beat in eggs and whip until light and fluffy. Add pumpkin and mix well. Sift together flour, soda, salt, baking powder, cinnamon and nutmeg. Add to pumpkin mixture. Stir until all dry ingredients are moistened. Add nuts and raisins and mix well. Grease 2 standard loaf pans with vegetable cooking spray. Divide equally the pumpkin mixture between the 2 pans and bake for 70 minutes. Remove from oven and leave loaves in pan for10 minutes before removing bread from pan. Cool finished loaves on rack prior to slicing.

VARIATIONS
◊ Dates make a nice substitute.

CARAMEL PUMPKIN BROWNIES

YIELD   8 SERVINGS

INGREDIENTS

Batter
1/8 Cup	Flour
1/2 Cup	Butter - unsalted
1 Cup	Brown Sugar - firm pack
1	Egg
1 1/2 tsp	Vanilla
1 Cup	Flour
1 tsp	Baking Powder
3/4 tsp	Cinnamon - ground
1/4 tsp	Salt
3/4 Cup	Pumpkin - canned
1/2 Cup	Pecans - chopped
1/4 Cup	Cream Cheese - softened
2 Tbls	Sugar
1	Egg Yolk
2 tsp	Heavy Cream

Caramel Sauce
5 Tbls	Butter - unsalted
1 Cup	Brown Sugar
2/3 Cup	Heavy Cream
1 tsp	Vanilla

8 Scoops	French Vanilla Ice Cream

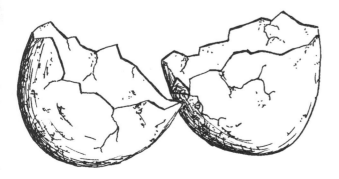

PREPARATION
Preheat oven to 350 degrees.

Caramel Sauce
In a heavy saucepan, over medium heat, melt butter. Add brown sugar and heavy cream and stir until sugar dissolves and comes to a boil. Boil for 5 minutes with out stirring. Remove from heat. Mix in vanilla and cool. This needs to be at room temperature for drizzling over brownies.

Batter
Set out cream cheese to obtain room temperature. Spray an 8-inch glass dish with vegetable spray and dust with $1/8$ cup of flour. Discard excess flour. Using an electric mixer, whip butter until light. Gradually add brown sugar and whip until it is blended well - about 2 minutes. Add 1 egg and 1 tsp of vanilla and whip to blend. Add flour, baking powder, cinnamon and salt and whip until well mixed. Whip in pumpkin. Stir in nuts and spread batter into prepared dish.

In a mixing bowl, combine cream cheese, 2 Tbls sugar, egg yolk, cream and remaining $1/2$ tsp of vanilla, mixing well. Drop cream cheese mixture by heaping tablespoons atop batter. Using a small knife, gently swirl cream cheese mixture into the batter creating a marbled pattern. Bake for 35 minutes or until a tester in the center of the brownies comes out clean. Remove from oven and set on rack to cool. After brownies are cooled drizzle caramel sauce over brownies using $1/3$ of the caramel sauce. Cut to desired size and serve with vanilla ice cream and top with the rest of the caramel sauce.

CRANBERRY NUT BREAD

Cooks Notes

YIELD   1 LOAF

INGREDIENTS

2 Cups	Flour
1 Cup	Sugar
1 1/2 tsp	Baking Powder
1/2 tsp	Baking Soda
1/2 tsp	Salt
1/4 Cup	Buttered Crisco
1	Orange - zest
3/4 Cup	Orange Juice
1	Egg
1 Cup	Fresh Cranberries - chopped
1/2 Cup	Walnuts - chopped

PREPARATION

Preheat oven to 350 degrees. In a mixing bowl, combine flour, sugar, baking powder, soda, salt and mix well. Using a grater, grate one whole orange creating the zest. In a separated mixing bowl, combine orange zest, juice, egg and mix well. Combine dry ingredients with juice and fold in cranberries and nuts. Spray 1 standard loaf pan with vegetable coating. Pour ingredients into loaf pan and bake for 70 minutes. Cool the bread for 10 minutes before removing from loaf pan, then cool on rack.

BUTTERNUT SQUASH

YIELD   **2 CUPS**

Cooks Notes

INGREDIENTS

2 Lb	Butternut Squash ◊
1/2 Cup	Butter - melted
3 Tbls	Brown Sugar
1/2 tsp	Salt
1/4 tsp	White Pepper - ground
1/2 tsp	Cinnamon - ground

PREPARATION

Preheat oven to 400 degrees. Cut squash in half and remove seeds. Place cut side down in a pan with about 1/4 inch of water and cover with foil. Cook for 30 minutes or until tender. Allow squash to cool after cooking and remove the skin. Place cooked squash pulp in a mixing bowl, add butter, 2 Tbls brown sugar, salt, pepper and cinnamon and mix well. Place in casserole dish and bake covered for 20 minutes at 350 degrees. Remove the cover, sprinkle remaining brown sugar on the top and bake uncovered for another 5 minutes.

VARIATIONS

◊ Other fall squash such as, Acorn or Buttercup may be used as well.

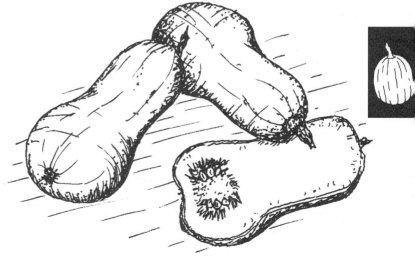

LUCILLE'S (SHINY) PUMPKIN PIE

YIELD	2 - 9" PIES

INGREDIENTS

Crust

2 Cups	Flour
1 tsp	Salt
12 Tbls	Crisco
6 Tbls	Water - cold

Batter

4	Eggs
1 - 29 oz Can	Pumpkin
1 1/2 Cups	Sugar
1 tsp	Salt
2 tsp	Cinnamon - ground
1 tsp	Nutmeg - ground
3 Cups	Evaporated Milk

Whipped Cream

3/4 Cup	Heavy Cream
1/2 tsp	Vanilla
1 tsp	Powdered Sugar

PREPARATION
Place small mixing bowl, in freezer for making whipped cream.

Cooks Notes

Crust
In a mixing bowl, combine flour and salt. Cut in shortening gradually adding 6 Tbls of cold water, mixing until all flour is moistened. Shape dough into a ball, divide in half and flatten to 1 inch thick. On a lightly floured board roll each dough ball into a circle, about 2 inches larger than the 9" pie pan. Line the pie pan with pie shell, turn edge under and flute if desired.

Batter
Preheat oven to 425 degrees. In a mixing bowl, combine all ingredients and mix well. Pour into pie shells. Bake in preheated oven for 15 minutes. Reduce temperature to 350 degrees and bake an additional 40-50 minutes.

Prepare whipped cream by placing heavy cream, vanilla and powdered sugar in the small mixing bowl chilled in the freezer, whip until stiff peak.

CARAMEL APPLE CAKE

YIELD   14 SERVINGS

INGREDIENTS

Batter
2 1/4 Cups	Sugar
1 1/2 Cup	Canola Oil
3	Eggs
3 Cups	Flour
1 tsp	Baking Soda
1/2 tsp	Salt
1/2 tsp	Cinnamon - ground
1/8 tsp	Nutmeg
3 Cups	Granny Smith Apples - chopped Δ
2 Cups	Pecans - chopped
2 tsp	Vanilla

Glaze
1 Cup	Brown Sugar
1/2 Cup	Butter - softened, unsalted
1/2 Cup	Heavy Cream

PREPARATION

Batter

Set out butter at room temperature to soften. Preheat oven to 350 degrees. In a large mixing bowl, whip sugar and oil together. Add eggs, one at a time. Sift dry ingredients and fold into the egg mixture. Stir in apples, pecans and vanilla. Pour batter in a greased 10-inch spring form pan. Bake for 1 hour or until tester comes out clean.

Glaze

Over high heat, in a saucepan, combine brown sugar, butter and cream. Bring to a boil and cook for 3 minutes, stirring constantly. Immediately after removing cake from oven pour glaze over entire cake. Let it cool thoroughly then remove from spring form pan. Slice into portions. Ready to serve.

CREAMED ONIONS

YIELD   8 SERVINGS

INGREDIENTS

4 Cups	Fresh Pearl Onions
4 Cups	White Cream Sauce (pg 208)
2 Tbls	Dry Sherry
2 Tbls	Fresh Lemon Juice
1 tsp	Paprika
2 Tbls	Fresh Parsley - chopped

PREPARATION

Preheat oven to 250 degrees. In a saucepan, blanch onions in boiling water until tender - about 5 minutes. Remove from heat and drain. In a mixing bowl, combine white cream sauce, sherry and lemon juice. Pour the cream sauce mixture on the onions and gently fold. Transfer finished product to a serving dish, sprinkle paprika on top. Cover and hold in oven until ready to serve. When ready to serve finish by garnishing with fresh parsley.

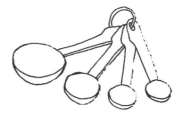

PECAN PIE

YIELD   1 9" PIE

INGREDIENTS

Crust
1 Cup	Flour
1/2 tsp	Salt
6 Tbls	Shortening
3 Tbls	Water - cold

Batter
1/2 Cup	Sugar
1 Cup	Dark Karo Syrup
1/4 tsp	Salt
1 Tbl	Flour
2	Eggs
1 1/4 Cups	Pecans - whole
1 tsp	Vanilla
1 Tbl	Butter - melted

Whipped Cream
3/4 Cup	Heavy Cream
1/2 tsp	Vanilla
1 tsp	Powdered Sugar

PREPARATION

Place small mixing bowl in freezer for making whipped cream.

Cooks Notes

Crust

In a mixing bowl, combine flour and salt. Cut in shortening gradually adding 3 Tbls of cold water, mixing until all flour is moistened. Shape dough into a ball, and flatten to 1 inch thick. On a lightly floured board roll dough ball into a circle, about 2 inches larger than the 9" pie pan. Line the pie pan with pie shell, turn edge under and flute if desired.

Batter

Preheat oven to 350 degrees. In a mixing bowl, combine sugar, syrup, salt, flour, and eggs mixing well. Melt butter, add vanilla and combine with batter adding $1^1/4$ cups pecan. Mix well and pour into the pie shell. Bake for 1 hour. Remove from oven, set on rack and allow it to cool, at least 30 minutes prior to cutting.

Prepare whipped cream by placing heavy cream, vanilla and powdered sugar in the small mixing bowl chilled in the freezer, whip until stiff peak.

PUMPKIN CAKE

YIELD	10 SERVINGS

INGREDIENTS

Batter

1	Egg
1/4 Cup	Vegetable Oil
1/2 Cup	Sugar
1/2 Cup	Pumpkin - canned
1/2 Cup	Flour
1/2 tsp	Baking Powder
1/4 tsp	Baking Soda
Titch	Salt
3/4 tsp	Cinnamon - ground
1/4 tsp	Nutmeg - ground

Frosting

3/4 oz	Cream Cheese - softened
1 1/2 Tbls	Butter - softened
1/4 Tbls	Whole Milk
1/4 tsp	Vanilla
3/4 Cup	Powdered Sugar
1/2 Cup	Walnuts - chopped

PREPARATION
Preheat oven to 375 degrees.
Set out, at room temperature cream cheese and butter to soften.

Cooks Notes

Batter
In a large mixing bowl, beat eggs, oil and sugar well. Add pumpkin and mix thoroughly. In a separate bowl, mix together flour, baking powder, soda, salt, cinnamon and nutmeg. Gradually add dry ingredients to the pumpkin mixture and mix until smooth. Pour into greased 9 by 11-inch cake pan. Bake for 20 minutes. Remove from oven, set on rack and cool before spreading frosting.

Frosting
In a mixing bowl, whip cream cheese until it has softened. Add butter mixing again until smooth. Stir in milk and vanilla. Gradually add powdered sugar and whip until smooth. Ready to spread on cooled cake. Top with chopped Walnuts.

SWEET POTATOES

Cooks Notes

YIELD   14 SERVINGS

INGREDIENTS

¹/4 Cup	Butter - softened
1 Cup	Brown Sugar - firm pack
¹/2 Cup	Pecans - chopped
¹/2 Cup	Dried Cherries
5 Lbs	Sweet Potatoes
4	Eggs
3 Tbls	Maple Syrup
2 Tbls	Vanilla
1 Tbl	Fresh Lemon Juice
2 tsp	Salt
2 Tbls	Butter - softened

PREPARATION

Set butter out at room temperature to soften. In a large soup pot, boil water and cook sweet potatoes until very tender - about 12 minutes. Drain and let set in a colander for 15 minutes. Preheat oven to 350 degrees. In a mixing bowl, combine ¹/4 cup softened butter, sugar, pecans and cherries. Mix well and set aside. In a mixing bowl, whip eggs, syrup, vanilla, lemon juice and salt. In a food processor, puree potatoes. Using 2 Tbls softened butter grease a casserole dish. Combine potatoes and sauce together and pour into casserole dish. Sprinkle pecans and dried cherries evenly over mixture. Bake until sweet potato mixture is set and topping bubbles - about 1 hour. Let stand for 15 minutes prior to serving.

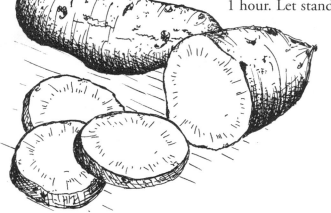

MARINATED CARROTS ♣

YIELD	12 SERVINGS

Cooks Notes

INGREDIENTS

3 Lbs	Baby Carrots
5 Cups	French Dressings (pg 211)
2 Tbls	Dill - fresh, chopped
3 Tbls	Fresh Parsley - chopped

PREPARATION

Chop parsley and dill and set aside. In a soup pot, boil enough water to submerge carrots completely. Fill a separate soup pot with enough water and ice to submerge carrots completely. Once obtaining a rolling boil add carrots and cook for 3 minutes or until just tender. Remove from heat, drain and immediately dump into ice water to stop the cooking process. After completely cooled, in a mixing bowl, combine carrots, dressing, dill and parsley. Mix well, cover and refrigerate overnight.

USES

A great dish for a Sunday Brunch or as a colorful garnish for any entrée.

PERFECT ENDINGS

"The world is so full of a number of things,
I'm sure we should all be as happy as kings."

-Robert Louis Stevenson

BAILEY'S BROWNIES

YIELD   LOTS

INGREDIENTS

1 Lb	Beef Liver
2	Eggs
1 Cup	Wheat Germ
1 Cup	Corn Meal
1 Tbl	Molasses
1 Tbl	Irish Cream Flavored Syrup
1 tsp	Garlic Salt
1 Tbl	Oil

PREPARATION

Preheat oven to 350 degrees. In a food processor, combine all ingredients and blend well. Place batter in a greased jelly-roll pan and bake for 25 minutes. Remove from oven, cool and cut into bars.

HINTS

If you have not figured it out by the name of this recipe, this is a treat for your four legged family members. However, as you can see by the ingredients, all family members may enjoy.

VARIATIONS

Depending on the individual whims of this family member, feel free to substitute chicken liver.

FRESH STRAWBERRIES CREAM ANGLAISE

YIELD   14 SERVINGS

INGREDIENTS

4 Cups	Whole Milk
1 tsp	Vanilla
1 1/4 Cup	Sugar
12	Eggs - yolks only
2 Qts	Fresh Strawberries ◊
14	Fresh Mint Leaves

Whipped Cream
3/4 Cup	Heavy Cream
1/2 tsp	Vanilla
1 tsp	Powdered Sugar

PREPARATION

Place small mixing bowl in freezer for making whipped cream. Wash strawberries, cut into slices and set aside. Separate yolks and set aside. In a saucepan, bring milk to a boil and reduce heat. In a mixing bowl, combine vanilla, sugar and egg yolks and mix vigorously. Add this mixture to milk and stir with a wooden spoon over heat creating a medium consistency and set aside. Prepare whipped cream by placing heavy cream, vanilla and powdered sugar in the small mixing bowl chilled in the freezer, whip until stiff peak. Using a red wine glass or similar dessert goblet fill 3/4 of glass with sliced strawberries. Cover completely with Cream Anglaise then top with a dollop of whipped cream. Garnish with a fresh mint leaf, now ready to serve

VARIATION

◊ Any fresh fruit works well with this recipe.

Cooks Notes

BREAD PUDDING WITH DRIED CHERRIES AND WHITE CHOCOLATE SAUCE ♣

YIELD	6 SERVINGS

INGREDIENTS

8 oz	French Bread - cut into 1-inch pieces
3 1/2 Cups	Heavy Cream
1 Cup	Milk
1/2 Cup	Sugar
1 Cup	Dried Cherries
18 oz	Bakers White Chocolate - pieces
7	Eggs - yolks
2	Eggs

Whipped Cream

3/4 Cup	Heavy Cream
1/2 tsp	Vanilla
1 tsp	Powdered Sugar

PREPARATION

Place small mixing bowl in freezer for making whipped cream. Preheat oven to 275 degrees. Arrange bread cubes on a sheet pan. Bake until light golden and dry - about 10 minutes. Transfer sheet pan to rack and cool completely. Increase oven temperature to 350 degrees. In a heavy large saucepan, combine 3 cups heavy cream, 1cup milk, and $1/2$ cup sugar. Bring to simmer over medium heat stirring until sugar dissolves. Remove from heat. Add 10 oz of white chocolate and stir until melted and smooth. In a mixing bowl, whip yolks and eggs vigorously. Gradually add warm chocolate mixture. Place bread cubes in a glass-baking dish. Add half of the chocolate mixture. Press bread cubes into chocolate mixture and set aside for 15 minutes. Gently mix in remaining chocolate mixture and dried cherries. Cover dish with foil. Bake pudding 45 minutes. Uncover and bake until top is golden brown, about 15 minutes. Transfer pudding to rack and cool slightly. Δ1 In a medium saucepan, bring remaining $1/2$-cup cream to a simmer. Remove saucepan, from heat and add remaining chocolate pieces and stir until melted and smooth. Prepare whipped cream by placing heavy cream, vanilla and powdered sugar in the small mixing bowl chilled in the freezer, whip until stiff peak. Top pudding with warm chocolate sauce and dollops of whipped cream.

HINTS

◊1 May be prepared one day ahead. Cover with foil and refrigerate. Re-heat covered in a 350-degree oven for 30 minutes.

Cooks Notes

LEMON POPPYSEED BISCUITS AND FRESH STRAWBERRIES

YIELD	6 SERVINGS

INGREDIENTS

Biscuits

1 1/2 Cups	Flour
5 Tbls	Sugar
1 1/2 tsp	Lemon Peel - grated
1 1/2 tsp	Baking Powder
1/4 tsp	Baking Soda
6 Tbls	Butter - unsalted
9 Tbls	Heavy Cream
2 Tbls	Fresh Lemon Juice
1 Tbl	Poppy Seeds

Strawberries

2 Pts	Strawberries - hulled
1/2 Cup	Maple Syrup
1/2 Cup	Sugar

Whipped Cream

3/4 Cup	Heavy Cream
1/2 tsp	Vanilla
1 tsp	Powdered Sugar

PREPARATION

Place small mixing bowl in freezer for making whipped
cream. Preheat oven to 350 degrees. In a mixer, add
flour, 3 Tbls of sugar, lemon peel, baking powder, baking
soda and salt. Add butter and by turning mixer on and
off create a rough mix. In a mixing bowl, add 8 Tbls of
heavy cream, lemon juice and poppy seeds and mix until
soft, moist dough forms. On a sheet pan evenly divide
mixture into a total of six biscuits. Using 1 Tbl of heavy
cream top biscuits. Sprinkle with 2 Tbls of sugar and
bake biscuits until golden brown - about 25 minutes.
After washing and hulling berries slice or mash and set
aside. In a mixing bowl, combine berries, sugar and
maple syrup and chill. Prepare whipped cream by placing
heavy cream, vanilla and powdered sugar in the small
mixing bowl chilled in the freezer, whip until stiff peak.
Serve at room temperature. Place biscuits in individual
dishes sliced and filled with strawberry mixture. Top with
whipped cream and serve.

Cooks Notes

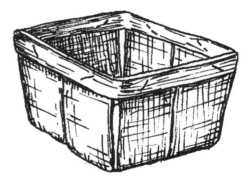

Hot Brandied Peaches

Yield   **12 Servings**

Ingredients

5 Lbs	Fresh Peaches ◊
1 Cup	Brandy
12 Scoops	French Vanilla Ice Cream

Simple Syrup
3 Cups	Water
3 Cups	Sugar

Whipped Cream
3/4 Cup	Heavy Cream
1/2 tsp	Vanilla
1 tsp	Powdered Sugar

Preparation

Place small mixing bowl in freezer for making whipped cream. In a saucepan, over high heat, boil water, add sugar, mix well and boil for 5 minutes making simple syrup. In a double boiler, combine peaches, and brandy, mixing well, and add simple syrup. Keep warm. Prepare whipped cream by placing heavy cream, vanilla and powdered sugar in the small mixing bowl chilled in the freezer, whip until stiff peak.

To Finish

Using a red wine glass or dessert goblet, place a scoop of ice cream and ladle the Brandied Peach mixture on top finishing with a dollop of whipped cream.

Variations

◊ IQF fruit can always be substituted. Be sure to thaw properly prior to using it in any recipe.

CARAMEL DIP AND FRESH FRUIT

Cooks Notes

YIELD 2 ¹/₂ CUPS

INGREDIENTS

1 Cup   Brown Sugar
¹/₄ Cup   Butter
1 Cup   Sour Cream

PREPARATION
In a saucepan, melt butter, add brown sugar and mix thoroughly. Let cool for 5 minutes. Add sour cream, mixing thoroughly. Set in refrigerator and chill for at least 2 hours.

HINTS
May be stored under refrigeration for up to one month

VARIATIONS
Any seasonal fresh fruit works well with this recipe. Great for apples, bananas & strawberries

USES
Cut fresh fruit into ¹/₄ - inch thick sections and place on large platter. Place dip in the center for dipping. Enjoy!

TURTLE BROWNIE

YIELD   12 SERVINGS

INGREDIENTS

Brownie

4 oz	Chocolate, unsweetened
1/2 Cup	Margarine
1 3/4 Cups	Sugar
3	Eggs
1 1/2 tsp	Salt
1 Cup	Flour
1 1/4 Cups	Pecan Pieces ◊
2 Tbls	Butter - softened
2 Tbls	Corn Syrup
1 Cup	Powdered Sugar
1 Tbl	Milk
1 tsp	Vanilla
1 Cup	Caramel Sauce Δ

Frosting

2 Tbls	Butter - unsalted
2 Tbls	Corn Syrup
1 Cup	Powdered Sugar
1 Tbl	Milk
1 tsp	Vanilla

Whipped Cream

3/4 Cup	Heavy Cream
1/2 tsp	Vanilla
1 tsp	Powdered Sugar

PREPARATION

Place small mixing bowl in freezer for making whipped cream. Prepare brownies by melting oven medium to low heat in a double boiler, 3oz chocolate and margarine. Add 1 $^1/_2$ cups granulated sugar. Preheat oven to 325 degrees. In a mixing bowl, blend together eggs, vanilla and salt then add the chocolate mixture and mix well. Add flour and mix well. Add $^1/_2$ cup of pecan pieces and fold into mixture. Pour batter into a greased 8-inch square pan and bake at 325 degrees for 40 minutes. Prepare Caramel Sauce per recipe. Keep warm and set aside. While brownies are baking make frosting by melting in a saucepan remaining chocolate and blending in softened butter and corn syrup. Then stir in powdered sugar, milk and vanilla, mixing well. Prepare whipped cream by placing heavy cream, vanilla and powdered sugar in the small mixing bowl chilled in the freezer, whip until stiff peak. Remove from oven and cool, about 40 minutes and top with frosting evenly sprinkle remaining pecan pieces on top and drizzle caramel over the top of the pecan pieces. Let brownies cool an additional 45 minutes, then cut into equal portions. Garnish with a dollop of whipped cream and ready to serve.

Cooks Notes

HINTS
Δ Refer to "Topping" recipe in Praline Ice Cream Pie. (pg 176)

VARIATIONS
◊ Any nut such as Walnuts, Macadamia Nuts, or Peanuts may be substituted.

PRALINE ICE CREAM PIE

YIELD   12 SERVINGS

INGREDIENTS

Topping
5 Tbls   Butter - unsalted
1 Cup   Brown Sugar
2/3 Cup   Heavy Cream
1 tsp   Vanilla

Cookies
12   Graham Crackers - whole
1 Cup   Butter - unsalted
1 Cup   Brown Sugar
1 1/2 Cups   Pecan Pieces

Crust
1 1/2 Cups   Graham Crackers crumbs
1/4 Cup   Butter - unsalted
1/4 Cup   Pecan Pieces

1/2 Gallon   French Vanilla Ice Cream

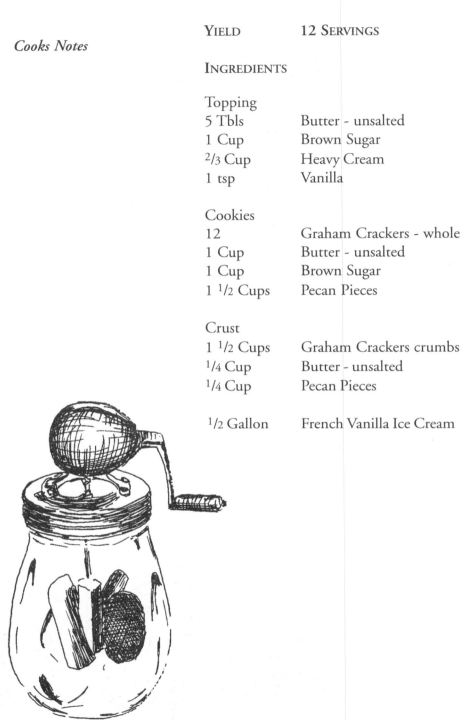

PREPARATION

Preheat oven to 350 degrees. Topping: In a heavy saucepan, over medium heat melt butter. Add brown sugar and heavy cream and stir until sugar dissolves and comes to a boil. Boil for 5 minutes with out stirring. Remove from heat. Mix in vanilla and cool.
Cookies: On a greased sheet pan place graham crackers tightly. In a medium saucepan, over medium heat, melt butter. Add brown sugar and stir until sugar dissolves and comes to a boil. Boil for 2 minutes without stirring. Remove from heat and add pecans, mixing completely. Spread this mixture evenly over graham crackers and bake until mixture bubbles - about 10 minutes. Remove cookies and cool. Remove ice cream from freezer.
Crust: In a medium saucepan, over medium heat, melt butter. Remove from heat and add graham crumbs and pecans and mix well. Grease a 9-inch spring form pan and press mixture in the bottom of the pan and bake 5 minutes. Remove from oven and cool. Break up 4 cookies and place on top of crust. Top with 1/4 of topping. Add 1/2 of the vanilla ice cream and spread evenly side to side creating a layer. Break up 4 cookies and place on top of ice cream. Add 1/4 of topping. Place the rest of the ice cream over topping and spread evenly side to side. Break up remaining cookies. Place on top of ice cream, top this with 1/4 of the topping. Freeze until firm.

HINTS

At the Inn we serve on a chilled plate, using the remaining topping, drizzled on top of the portioned pie and then top with a dollop of whipped cream and serve.

Cooks Notes

WHITE CHOCOLATE CAKE AND RASPBERRY SAUCE ♣

YIELD	12 SERVINGS

INGREDIENTS

Batter

2 - 8 oz Pkg	White Chocolate Morsels
1 1/2 Cups	Butter - unsalted
1 Cup	Sugar
1 Cup	Heavy Cream
1 Tbl	Vanilla
1/2 tsp	Salt
8	Eggs

Raspberry Sauce

1 Cup	Water
1/2 Cup	Sugar
1 1/2 Cup	Fresh Raspberries ◊

Glaze

20 oz	White Chocolate Morsels
1 1/2 Cups	Heavy Cream
1/4 Cup	Light Corn Syrup

Whipped Cream

3/4 Cup	Heavy Cream
1/2 tsp	Vanilla
1 tsp	Powdered Sugar

PREPARATION

Preheat oven to 350 degrees.

Batter

Grease a 10-inch spring form pan. In a double boiler, over low heat combine white chocolate, butter, cream, vanilla and salt. Stir frequently until chocolate is fully melted and mixture is smooth. Remove from heat. In a mixing bowl, whip eggs slightly and slowly add chocolate mixture until well blended. Pour this batter into the

spring form pan and spread evenly. Bake for 55 minutes
or until tester, placed 2 inches from the edge, comes out
clean. Remove from oven and cool cake completely on a
wire rack. Remove the sides of spring form pan leaving
the cake on the base. Wrap and refrigerate.

Cooks Notes

Next Day
Raspberry Sauce
In a saucepan, over high heat, combine ingredients and
stir for 12-15 minutes and remove from heat. Cool for
20 minutes. Pour this mixture into a food processor and
puree. Pour this mixture through a strainer to remove
raspberry seed.

Glaze
Place small mixing bowl in freezer for making whipped
cream. In a heavy saucepan, over low heat, combine the
heavy cream and corn syrup. Bring to a simmer. Slowly
whisk in white chocolate and mix until smooth. Transfer
this to a mixing bowl and whip occasionally, then let sit
at room temperature for 4 hours. Remove cake from
spring form base and cover the entire cake with glaze.
Using a spoon, drop small dots of raspberry sauce on
the top of the cake. With a knife, swirl the raspberry
sauce into frosting, creating a marble look. Refrigerate
for 1 hour.
Prepare whipped cream by placing heavy cream, vanilla
and powdered sugar in the small mixing bowl chilled
in the freezer, whip until stiff peak. On dessert plates,
drizzle raspberry sauce on the outer edge and place the
cake in the center of the plate. Top with a dollop of
whipped cream.

VARIATIONS
◊ IQF fruit can always be substituted. Be sure to thaw
properly prior to using it in any recipe.

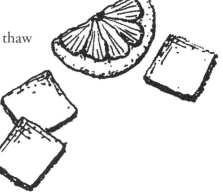

CHOCOLATE MOUSSE CAKE ♣

Cooks Notes

YIELD   12 SERVINGS

INGREDIENTS

Batter
2 (8oz pkg)	Semi-Sweet Chocolate Morsels
2 Cups	Butter - unsalted
1 Cup	Sugar
1 Cup	Half & Half
1 Tbl	Vanilla
1/2 tsp	Salt
8	Eggs

Glaze
1 Cup	Semi-Sweet Chocolate Morsels
2 Tbls	Butter

Whipped Cream
3/4 Cup	Heavy Cream
1/2 tsp	Vanilla
1 tsp	Powdered Sugar

PREPARATION
Batter

Preheat oven to 350 degrees. Grease a 10-inch spring form pan. In a large heavy saucepan, over low heat, combine semi-sweet chocolate, butter, sugar, half & half, vanilla and salt, stirring frequently until chocolate is fully melted and mixture is smooth. Remove from heat. In a mixing bowl, beat eggs slightly and slowly add chocolate mixture until well blended. Pour this batter into the spring form pan and spread evenly. Bake for 45 minutes, or until tester comes out clean 2-inches from the center of the cake, remove from oven and cool, about 1 hour. Carefully remove cake from spring form pan, wrap and refrigerate over night.

Next Day
Glaze

In a heavy saucepan, over low heat, combine chocolate and butter, stirring frequently until smooth. Remove from heat and cool for 1/2 hour.

To Finish

Place small mixing bowl in freezer for making whipped cream. Prepare whipped cream by placing heavy cream, vanilla and powdered sugar in the small mixing bowl chilled in the freezer, whip until stiff peak. Spread glaze smoothly over entire cake and down the sides and refrigerate until you are ready to portion. Place a slice in the center of a dessert plate and garnish with a dollop of whipped cream.

Cooks Notes

CHOCOLATE CHEESE CAKE ♣

YIELD	12-16 SERVINGS

INGREDIENTS

Crust
1/4 Cup	Butter - melted
1 Cup	Sliced Almonds - toasted ◊
1 8 1/2 oz Pkg	Thin Chocolate Wafers ◊

Batter
4 Cups	Cream Cheese - softened
2 Cups	Sugar
4	Eggs
1/2 Cups	Chocolate Chips ◊
1 Tbl	Unsweetened Cocoa Powder ◊
1 tsp	Vanilla
2 Cups	Sour Cream

Whipped Cream
3/4 Cup	Heavy Cream
1/2 tsp	Vanilla
1 tsp	Powdered Sugar

Topping
1/4 Cup	Heavy Cream
1/2 Cup	Semi-Sweet Chocolate Morsels ◊

PREPARATION

Set cream cheese out at room temperature to soften. Preheat oven at 350 degrees. Evenly spread sliced almonds on a sheet pan and place in oven for about 5 minutes or until almonds are toasted. Remove and cool

Crust

In a saucepan, melt butter. In a food processor, combine melted butter, chocolate wafers and 1/2 cup of almonds and process until completely ground. Press this mixture into a 10-inch spring form pan and chill.

Batter

In a large mixing bowl, whip cream cheese until light and fluffy. Gradually add sugar. Add eggs, one at a time, and beat well until batter is smooth. Add melted chocolate, cocoa and vanilla extract. Add in sour cream. Pour cream cheese mixture into chilled 10-inch spring form pan. Bake for 1 hour 10 minutes or until all but a 2-inch diameter in the center of the cheesecake has set. Remove from oven and cool at room temperature for at least 45 minutes prior to refrigeration. Chill overnight.

Next Day
Topping

Place small mixing bowl in freezer for making whipped cream. In a saucepan, over medium heat, bring heavy cream to a simmer. Add chocolate morsels and mix until smooth. Cool for at least 20 minutes. Prepare whipped cream by placing heavy cream, vanilla and powdered sugar in the small mixing bowl chilled in the freezer, whip until stiff peak.

To Finish

Remove cheesecake from spring form pan and set in the center of your serving plate. Drizzle chocolate topping over entire cake and sprinkle remaining almonds. Apply dollops of whipped cream on each slice. Ready to serve.

VARIATIONS

◊ The flavor of the cake can be changed based on the flavor morsels, wafers and nuts used.

Cooks Notes

BAILEY'S IRISH CRÈME CHOCOLATE PATÉ ♣

YIELD   1 LOAF

INGREDIENTS

Batter
3/4 Cup   Fresh Brewed Coffee
1/4 Cup   Bailey's Irish Crème Liquor ◊1
1 Cup   Sugar
1 Lb   Semi-Sweet Chocolate Morsels
1/2 Lb   Butter - unsalted
8   Eggs

Topping
1 Cup   Water
1/2 Cup   Sugar
1 1/2 Cup   Fresh Raspberries ◊2

Whipped Cream
3/4 Cup   Heavy Cream
1/2 tsp   Vanilla
1 tsp   Powdered Sugar

PREPARATION

Set butter out at room temperature to soften. Preheat oven at 350 degrees.

Batter

In a saucepan, over medium heat, combine coffee and Bailey's and get hot. Add sugar and stir until it dissolves into a light syrup. Stir in chocolate slowly until chocolate is melted and mixture is smooth. Remove from heat and cool 20 minutes. Add in softened butter and mix well. Add in eggs, one at a time, and beat until creamy and smooth. Using a vegetable spray, spray the inside of a standard loaf pan. Pour in batter. In a pan large enough to hold the loaf pan with at least 2-inch sides place the loaf pan in a bath of water and bake for 1 hour. Remove from oven and set on rack cooling for one hour. Chill over night.

Topping

In a saucepan, over high heat, combine ingredients and stir for 12-15 minutes and remove from heat. Cool for 20 minutes. Pour this mixture into a food processor and puree. Pour this mixture through a strainer to remove raspberry seed.

To Finish

Place small mixing bowl in freezer for making whipped cream. Using a dessert plate drizzle this topping on the plate so that when the paté is placed in the center you will have raspberry sauce exposed. Remove paté from loaf pan by using a heated knife and placing it between the paté and the pan, separating the paté from the loaf pan. Cut the slices 1/2 inch thick and place in the center of the dessert plate. Prepare whipped cream by placing heavy cream, vanilla and powdered sugar in the small mixing bowl chilled in the freezer, whip until stiff peak. Garnish with a dollop of whipped cream.

VARIATIONS

◊1 Other liquors or flavor morsels may be substituted to create a signature Paté of your own. ◊2 IQF fruit can always be substituted. Be sure to thaw properly prior to using it in any recipe

APPLE MOUND

YIELD	12 SERVINGS

INGREDIENTS

$^1/_3$ Lb	Butter - unsalted
$^1/_3$ Lb	Sugar
1 Tbl	Cinnamon
5 Lbs	Fresh Apples ◊
12 Scoops	French Vanilla Ice Cream

Simple Syrup
3 Cups	Water
3 Cups	Sugar

Whipped Cream
$^3/_4$ Cup	Heavy Cream
$^1/_2$ tsp	Vanilla
1 tsp	Powdered Sugar

PREPARATION

Place small mixing bowl in freezer for making whipped cream. In a saucepan, over high heat, boil water, add sugar, mix well and boil for 5 minutes. In a heavy sauce pan, combine butter, sugar and cinnamon, add simple syrup and boil 5 minutes. Remove from heat and add apples, mixing well. Keep warm. Place a small mixing bowl in freezer for making whipped cream. Prepare whipped cream by placing heavy cream, vanilla and powdered sugar in the small mixing bowl chilled in the freezer, whip until stiff peak.

Cooks Notes

To Finish

Using a red wine glass or dessert goblet, place in a scoop of ice cream and ladle the Apple Mound mixture on top finishing with a dollop of whipped cream.

VARIATIONS

◊ IQF fruit can always be substituted. Be sure to thaw properly prior to using it in any recipe. With the addition of a short cake biscuit under the ice cream makes this dessert a meal.

LEMON ICE CREAM WHITE CHOCOLATE TARTUFO ♣

YIELD	12 SERVINGS

INGREDIENTS

2 Pints	Schwan's Glacier Bay Lemon Yogurt
1 1/2 Pints	French Vanilla Ice Cream
1 1/2 Cups	Sliced Almonds - toasted
1	Lemon - sliced

Lemon Curd
1/2 Cup	Fresh Lemon Juice
3	Eggs Yolks - beaten
1 Cup	Sugar
6 Tbls	Butter - unsalted
1	Lemon - zest

White Chocolate Glaze
1 Cup	Heavy Cream
2 Tbls	Light Corn Syrup
2 Cups	White Chocolate Morsels

Whipped Cream
3/4 Cup	Heavy Cream
1/2 tsp	Vanilla
1 tsp	Powdered Sugar

PREPARATION

Preheat oven to 350 degrees. On a sheet pan spread evenly, sliced almonds and bake for 5 minutes or until almonds are toasted. Place small mixing bowl in freezer for making whipped cream. Place butter at room temperature to soften.

Lemon Curd
Prepare set by grating the lemon peel creating the zest of the lemon and set aside. In a mixing bowl, whisk egg yolks and lemon zest until completely mixed. In a double boiler, combine lemon juice, butter, and sugar and mix until dissolved. Remove the top of the double boiler from

heat and slowly add to the egg and lemon mixture, mixing well. Return to double boiler stir constantly, about 15 minutes or until the curd is thick and sticks to the back of the wooden spoon. Chill for 1 hour.

To Finish
Set yogurt out at room temperature to soften. Line a standard loaf pan with plastic wrap leaving a 3 - inch overhang on all sides. Using a small rubber spatula spread softened yogurt evenly in the pan being sure to cover completely side to side. Freeze until firm, - about one hour. Remove from freezer and spread $1/2$ cup of lemon curd on top of the lemon yogurt. Top this with $1/2$ cup of almonds and refreeze for $1/2$ hour.

White Chocolate Glaze
In a heavy saucepan, combine heavy cream and corn syrup and get hot. Remove from heat and add white chocolate. Mix until melted and smooth. Remove from heat and cool to room temperature - about 45 minutes, whisking occasionally.

Set ice cream out at room temperature to soften. Remove loaf pan from freezer and with a rubber spatula, spread the ice cream evenly and refreeze for 1 hour.

Remove from freezer and spread $2/3$ of the white chocolate glaze on the top of the ice cream and refreeze for 2 hours. Line a sheet pan with parchment paper and with a warm knife separate the ice cream from the loaf pan and invert loaf pan on sheet pan. Remove plastic wrap. Working very quickly spread the rest of the white chocolate glaze on the top and sides of the loaf. Sprinkle remaining almonds on top and sides and refreeze for 1 hour. Slice lemon and set aside. Prepare whipped cream by placing heavy cream, vanilla and powdered sugar in the small mixing bowl chilled in the freezer, whip until stiff peak. Prepare dessert plates by drizzling left over lemon curd and white chocolate decoratively on the plate. Cut slices $1/2$ inch thick then cut again in half diagonally. Creating two triangle pieces. Place on dessert plate, topped with a dollop of whipped cream and a twisted slice of fresh lemon and serve.

BUTTERSCOTCH NUT COOKIES

YIELD	5 DOZ

INGREDIENTS

3/4 Cup	Margarine
1 Pkg (6oz)	Butterscotch Morsels ◊1
1 tsp	Baking Soda
2 Tbls	Boiling Water
3/4 Cup	Sugar
1 Cup	Flour
2 Cups	Oatmeal - uncooked
1/2 tsp	Salt
1/4 Cup	Walnuts - chopped ◊2

PREPARATION
Preheat oven to 350 degrees. Using a double boiler, melt margarine and butterscotch morsels. Stir in soda and boiling water, mix completely then add all remaining ingredients. Remove from heat and cool. Using a greased sheet pan place one inch balls two inches apart. Bake for 10-15 minutes. Remove cookies to a rack and cool.

HINTS
Should be stored in a tightly covered container.

VARIATIONS
◊1 Any flavored morsel - dark chocolate, white chocolate or milk chocolate may be substituted. ◊ 2 May substitute your favorite nut or dried cherries to make this particular recipe real special.

RECIPES REVISITED

"Whoe'er has travell'd life's dull round,
Where'er his stages might have been,
May sigh to think he still has found
The warmest welcome, at an inn." William
Shenstone

CORN CASSEROLE

Cooks Notes

YIELD   6 SERVINGS

INGREDIENTS

15 $^1/_2$ oz Can	Whole Kernel Corn
15 $^1/_2$ oz Can	Cream Style Corn
8 $^1/_2$ oz Box	Jiffy Corn Muffin Mix
1 Cup	Sour Cream
$^1/_4$ Lb	Butter

PREPARATION

Melt butter and add undrained whole kernel and cream style corn, muffin mix and sour cream, mixing well. Pour into a 1 $^1/_2$ qt flat casserole. Bake at 350 degrees for 45 minutes, until top is brown and center is firm.

CHEESE WOOKIES

YIELD   150 WOOKIES

Cooks Notes

INGREDIENTS

1/2 Lb	Butter - softened
1/2 Lb	Margarine - softened
1 Lb	Sharp Cheddar Cheese - shredded
4 Cups	Flour
	Salt

PREPARATION

In a mixing bowl, combine softened butter, softened margarine, shredded cheese and flour, mixing well. Refrigerate dough for one hour. Roll dough into round balls the diameter of a nickel. Place on a cookie sheet pan and bake at 325 degrees for 25 minutes. Remove from oven, place wookies on brown paper on countertop and very lightly salt. Allow to cool and serve.

HINTS

May be stored, sealed, under refrigeration for up to two weeks.

VARIATIONS

Grandma's original recipe called for almond slices and egg whites. To try the original version, slightly flatten wookies with thumb before baking, place almond slice on flattened wookie top, brush top with beaten egg white, then bake and finish as above.

SWISS ONION SOUP

YIELD   5 CUPS

INGREDIENTS

2 Cups	Water
5 Tbls	Butter
1 tsp	Garlic Puree
3 Cups	Onion - thinly sliced
3/4 tsp	Dry Mustard
1/2 tsp	Salt
3 Tbls	Flour
1 1/2 Cups	Milk - scalded
1 1/2 Cups	Swiss Cheese - shredded
1/2 tsp	Horseradish
1 Tbl	Dry Sherry
1/2 tsp	Black Pepper - ground
1/2 tsp	Soy Sauce
3 Drops	Tabasco Sauce
2 Shakes	Worcestershire Sauce

PREPARATION

In a saucepan, combine water, 2 Tbls butter, garlic puree, onion slices, mustard and salt; cover and simmer over low heat, until onions are tender, about 20 minutes. Scald milk. In a separate saucepan, make a roux by melting remaining 3 Tbl butter and stirring in flour, cooking while stirring over low heat for 5 minutes. Add scalded milk to roux Δ, mixing well to make a medium thick cream sauce. Then slowly add shredded cheese to sauce, mixing until melted. Add horseradish and sherry to cheese sauce and combine the cheese sauce with contents of saucepan containing onions, mixing thoroughly. Mix in pepper, soy, Tabasco and Worcestershire sauces.

HINTS

Δ Scalded milk must be hot when added to the roux, to make cream sauce thicken quickly.

This soup may be stored frozen, sealed, for 2 -3 months.

APPLE BREAD STUFFING

YIELD	4 CUPS

Cooks Notes

INGREDIENts

4 Cups	Dried Bread Cubes (¹/4") Δ ◊
2 Cups	Water
4 tsp	Wyler's Chicken Bouillon
1 Cup	Onions - diced
1 Cup	Celery - diced
2 Cups	Apples - sliced
1 Tbl	Cinnamon - ground
1 Tbl	Poultry Seasoning

PREPARATION

In a deep sauce pan or soup pot, mix water and chicken bouillon; then add onions, celery, apples, cinnamon and poultry seasoning, and bring to a boil. Add bread cubes, stir thoroughly, cool and refrigerate until ready to use.

HINTS

This stuffing will keep under refrigeration for up to two weeks, or can be frozen and held for up to six months. When using frozen stuffing, allow to thaw, and check moisture content - a small addition of water may be necessary. Δ Vary the amount of bread used to increase or decrease the moistness of the stuffing.

VARIATIONS

◊ Herbed, rye, or whole wheat bread may be used to vary the flavor.
The addition of dried tart cherries gives this stuffing another dimension.

USES

This stuffing is used for poultry or pork, including chops, crown roasts, and rolled roasts.

LEMON BUTTER SAUCE

YIELD   1^1/$_2$ CUPS

INGREDIENTS

1 Cup	Fresh Lemon Juice
1 Lb	Butter - cubed

PREPARATION
Bring lemon juice to a boil and remove from heat. Place butter, cut into small pieces, into the lemon juice a piece at a time and stir vigorously Δ until melted.

HINTS
May be stored under refrigeration for up to one month or frozen for at least six months. However, will not work by itself as a sauce after storage, see Uses.
Δ For a smoother and thicker sauce, use a high speed hand held mixer: you cannot over mix this sauce.

VARIATIONS
Add favorite seasonings to create a personal sauce: fresh basil for a lemon basil butter, capers for a great piccata sauce, pecan pieces for a lemon pecan butter sauce.

USES
As a freshly prepared sauce, use with vegetables, poultry and fish. After refrigerated or frozen storage, it may be used as the base for another batch of this sauce, by addition of more fresh lemon juice and butter, or may be used as is to replace butter in several recipes, wherever you would like a bit of lemon flavor.

GARLIC BUTTER SAUCE

YIELD   2^1/$_2$ CUPS

INGREDIENTS

1 Lb	Butter - softened
^{1}/$_8$ tsp	White Pepper - ground
1 Tbl	Garlic Puree
2 tsp	Anchovy Paste
2 Tbls	Fresh Parsley - chopped
2 Tbls	Green Pepper - finely chopped
2 Tbls	Red Pepper - finely chopped
^{1}/$_4$ Cup	Dry White Wine ◊

PREPARATION
Soften butter by letting it sit out at room temperature for
at least 2 hours. In a power mixing bowl, add all ingredients except wine and mix well. Slowly add the wine and
mix until the wine has been completely absorbed Δ by
the butter and the sauce peaks.

HINTS
May be frozen for storage, for up to six months, or
refrigerated for up to one month.
Δ It is important that the wine be well mixed to prevent
later separation.

VARIATIONS
◊ For use with red meats, replace the dry white wine
with a dry red wine.

USES
May be used for sautéing nearly anything, as a spread on
French or Italian loaves, or as a base sauce for escargot.

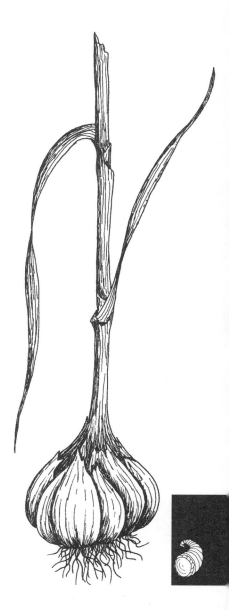

ALMONDINE BREADING

YIELD   2 ¼ CUPS

INGREDIENTS

2 Cups	Dried Bread Crumbs Δ
1	Lemon - zest only, finely grated
½ Cup	Almonds - sliced

PREPARATION
Thoroughly mix all ingredients.

HINTS
May be stored under refrigeration for 1-2 months.
Δ This breading requires very fine bread crumbs. If 'Japanese style', i.e. coarse crumbs, are available, process for 1 or 2 minutes in a food processor to reduce the size of the crumb.

USES
This breading is used with any pan-fried or oven-baked fish.

RICE PILAF

YIELD   4 CUPS

INGREDIENTS

1 ¹/₂ Cup	Long Grain White Rice ◊1
3 Cups	Water
1 ¹/₂ tsp	Wyler's Chicken Bouillon
1 ¹/₂ tsp	Wyler's Beef Bouillon
6 Tbls	Butter
¹/₄ Cup	Onions - finely chopped ◊2

PREPARATION

In a small mixing bowl, combine chicken & beef bouillon with water, mix well and set aside. In a sauté pan, melt 3 Tbls butter, add chopped onions and sauté until tender. Preheat oven to 375 degrees. In a large casserole dish, place uncooked rice, add sautéed onions and mix well Δ. Add bouillon and water mixture, mix well, bring to a boil on stove. Then cover with foil, cut two or three slits in the foil and bake 18 minutes at 375 degrees. Remove foil and mix in the remaining butter.

HINTS

Δ To assure an even mixture of onions and rice, add bouillion and water mixture only after pre-mixing rice and onions.

VARIATIONS

◊1 Brown rice may be substituted for white rice, or a mixture of wild and brown or white rices will produce an interesting pilaf.
◊2 Shallots and/or leeks may be substituted for the onions.
To spice up this rice, add a touch of sherry to the bouillon/water mixture.

Orchard Chicken

Cooks Notes

Yield   **6 Servings**

Ingredients

6 - 6 oz	Chicken Breasts - skinless & boneless ◊
2 tsp	Thyme Leaf, chopped
2 tsp	Poultry Seasoning
3 Cups	Apple Bread Stuffing (Pg 195)
1 Cups	Dried Cherry Glaze (Pg 209)
3 Cups	Rice Pilaf (Pg 199)
2 Tbls	Fresh Parsley - chopped

PREPARATION

With a tenderizing mallet, pound chicken breasts flat, using care to avoid tearing the meat. Preheat oven to 375 degrees. Prepare Rice Pilaf Δ. Lay each breast on a work surface with the inside of the breast facing up. Place $1/2$ cup Apple Bread Stuffing in the center of each breast. Fold tail end of breast up and over the stuffing, fold each side of the breast up and over the stuffing, then invert the breast onto a baking pan. Sprinkle thyme and poultry seasoning on the top of the stuffed breasts. Bake chicken breasts and Rice Pilaf in preheated oven at 375 degrees for 20 minutes. In a small saucepan, warm Dried Cherry Glaze. Prepare each dinner plate by placing $1/2$ cup of Rice Pilaf in the center of the plate, making a nest. Place stuffed breast in the nest and place 3 Tbls warmed Dried Cherry Glaze on each breast, then sprinkle with chopped parsley and serve.

HINTS

Δ Rice Pilaf may be prepared, but not baked, at this point. It may be cooked along with the chicken breasts, as the baking times and temperatures are nearly identical.

VARIATIONS

◊ Chicken breasts may be replaced with thick cut pork chops, with Apple Bread Stuffing placed in pockets cut into the chops.

CRAB MEAT STUFFED CHICKEN BREAST

YIELD   6 SERVINGS

INGREDIENTS

6 - 6 oz	Chicken Breasts - skinless & boneless ◊
2 tsp	Thyme Leaf
2 tsp	Poultry Seasoning
3 Cups	Crab Meat Stuffing (Pg 207)
3/4 Cup	Lemon Butter Sauce (Pg 196)
1/4 Cup	Pecan Pieces
3 Cups	Rice Pilaf (Pg 199)
2 Tbls	Fresh Parsley - chopped

PREPARATION

With a tenderizing mallet, pound chicken breasts flat,
using care to avoid tearing the meat. Preheat oven to 375
degrees. Prepare Rice Pilaf Δ. Lay each breast on a work
surface with the inside of the breast facing up. Place $1/2$
cup Crab Meat Stuffing in the center of each breast. Fold
tail end of breast up and over the stuffing, fold each side
of the breast up and over the stuffing then invert the
breast onto a baking pan. Sprinkle thyme and poultry
seasoning on the top of the stuffed breasts. Bake chicken
breasts and Rice Pilaf, in preheated oven at 375 degrees
for 20 minutes. In a small saucepan, combine Lemon
Butter Sauce and pecan pieces to make Lemon Pecan
Butter Sauce. Prepare each dinner plate by placing $1/2$
cup of Rice Pilaf in the center of the plate, making a
nest. Place stuffed breast in the nest and place 3 Tbls
Lemon Pecan Butter Sauce on each breast, then sprinkle
with chopped parsley and serve.

HINTS

Δ Rice Pilaf may be prepared, but not baked, at this
point. It may be cooked along with the chicken breasts,
as the baking times and temperatures are nearly identical.

VARIATIONS

◊ Chicken breasts may be replaced with Schrod, Sole, or
Whitefish. In the case of Schrod or Whitefish, a pocket
may be cut into the fillet; with Sole, two fillets may be
used as top and bottom with stuffing between.

TURKEY 'POT' PIE

YIELD   12 - 14 SERVINGS

INGREDIENTS

5 $^{1}/_{3}$ Cups	Milk
1 Cup	Butter
$^{2}/_{3}$ Cup	Flour
2 $^{1}/_{2}$ tsp	Wyler's Chicken Bouillon
2 $^{1}/_{2}$ Cups	Water
2 $^{1}/_{2}$ Cups	Onions - diced $^{1}/_{4}$ inch
2 $^{1}/_{2}$ Cups	Celery - diced $^{1}/_{4}$ inch
2 $^{1}/_{2}$ Cups	Carrots - diced $^{1}/_{4}$ inch
1 tsp	Thyme - fresh, chopped
1 tsp	White Pepper - ground
1 tsp	Salt
1 tsp	Poultry Seasoning
2 $^{1}/_{2}$ Lbs	Turkey Meat - cubed $^{1}/_{4}$ inch Δ1 ◊1
1 Box	Pepperidge Farm Puff Pastry Sheets Δ2
1	Egg
2 Tbls	Water

PREPARATION

Prepare a cream sauce by scalding milk in a small sauce pan. In a separate sauce pan make a roux by melting $^{2}/_{3}$ cup butter, heating to a foam, without burning, then stirring in flour. Continue to stir and cook roux for 5 minutes over medium heat. Add scalded milk and stir until sauce is thick and of smooth consistency. Set aside. In a large soup pot mix water and chicken bouillon. Add

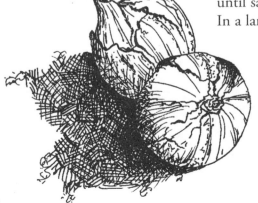

$1/3$ cup butter heating until butter is melted. Add diced onions, celery, carrots, thyme leaf, pepper, salt, and poultry seasoning; cover and cook for 15 minutes; being careful to leave the vegetables a little crisp. Preheat oven to 375 degrees. Add cooked cubed turkey meat and cream sauce; mixing well. Divide mixture between two 9 inch x 13 inch casserole dishes Δ3 ◊2. Cover each dish with a sheet of puff pastry. In a small mixing bowl, beat egg and 2 Tbls water together to make an egg wash. Brush top of pastry sheets. Bake for 20 minutes at 375 degrees or until the pastry browns.

Cooks Notes

HINTS

Δ1 Use leftover cooked turkey, or, if cooking the turkey for this recipe, place turkey in soup pot, cover with water, and add 2 bay leaves, some celery, onion, and carrots, then bring water to a boil, reduce heat and simmer breast meat for about 45 minutes, remove from water, chill and cube.

Δ 2 This puff pastry can be found at many food stores, in the freezer section. One box contains 2 sheet, each 14 inches by 11 inches.

Δ 3 At this point, mixture may be stored, sealed, under refrigeration for up to seven days before cooking and serving. If cooking after refrigerated storage, bake at 350 degrees for 45 minutes.

VARIATIONS

◊1 You may substitute cubed cooked beef or pork, replacing chicken bouillion with beef bouillon and omitting poultry seasoning.

◊2 You may make individual pot pies by using oven proof soup crocks, filling with the pot pie mixture, cutting puff pastry sheets to fit crock tops, and baking individually at 350 degrees for 20 minutes.

BÉARNAISE SAUCE

YIELD	1 ¹/₂ CUPS

INGREDIENTS

1 Tbl	Black Peppercorns - crushed
¹/₄ Cup	Tarragon Vinegar
1 Cup	Drawn Butter Δ1
4	Egg Yolks
1/2 tsp	Tarragon - fresh, chopped
1 Tbl	Fresh Lemon Juice
¹/₈ tsp	Salt
Titch	Cayenne Pepper ◊

PREPARATION

Crush peppercorns with a rolling pin. In a sauce pan, combine crushed pepper with vinegar and cook until the volume has been reduced by half. Remove from heat and strain into a blender. With blender at a medium setting add warmed drawn butter very, very slowly. (The drawn butter should be warmed to prevent the sauce from breaking.) Add egg yolks, one at a time. Add lemon juice and a titch of cayenne pepper. Add tarragon and salt. Remove and place in a stainless steel bowl at room temperature. Δ2 Use immediately, do not attempt to store.

HINTS

Δ1 To make drawn butter, melt butter, allow solids to settle, and carefully pour off liquid. This liquid is drawn butter, and may be cooled and stored for later use. Plan to lose 25 - 35 percent of the beginning volume.
Δ2 If the sauce breaks at this point, add an ice cube to the mixture and stir vigorously. The sauce should return to the proper consistency.

VARIATIONS

◊ Cayenne pepper may be replaced with 4 drops of Tabasco sauce.

USES

Use with flavorful fish and seafood or beef encrutes.

CRAB MEAT STUFFING

YIELD   4 CUPS

INGREDIENTS

2 Cups	Crab Meat Δ1 ◊1
1/2 Cup	Drawn Butter Δ2
1/2 Cup	Onions - finely chopped
3/4 Cup	Bread Crumbs ◊2
1 1/2 Cup	White Cream Sauce (pg 212)

PREPARATION

In a sauté pan, heat butter, add onions and sauté until
tender. Set aside to cool Δ3. Add cool cream sauce, cool
onions, crab meat and bread crumbs and mix well.
Refrigerate and allow to set up, approximately one hour.

HINTS

May be stored, well sealed, under refrigeration for 7-10
days; or frozen for 1-2 months.
Δ1 Be careful to remove any cartilage from the crab meat
you buy.
Δ2 To make drawn butter, melt butter, allow solids to settle, and carefully pour off liquid. This liquid is drawn
butter, and may be cooled and stored for later use. Plan
to lose 25-35 percent of the beginning volume.
Δ3 It is very important that hot and cold items are not
mixed together as this can cause the stuffing to sour.

VARIATIONS

◊1 We use Chesapeak Bay Blue Crab - it is a sweet crab.
King Crab, Stone Crab or another favorite of yours may
be used as well. Avoid imitation crab!
◊2 We use plain bread crumbs in this stuffing. Feel free
to use herbal or seasoned crumbs if you prefer. Keep in
mind, however, that the stuffing should not have an over-
powering flavor.

USES

This stuffing is used in several freshwater and ocean fishes, shellfish, and shrimp; also stuffed mushroom caps.

HERBAL BREADING

Cooks Notes

YIELD   3 CUPS

INGREDIENTS

2 ³/4 Cups	Dried Bread Crumbs Δ
¹/4 Lb	Romano Cheese - grated
1 Tbl	Thyme - fresh, chopped
1 Tbl	Basil - fresh, chopped
1 Tbl	Oregano - fresh, chopped
1 Tbl	Garlic Puree
2 Tbls	Fresh Parsley - chopped

PREPARATION
Thoroughly mix all ingredients.

HINTS
May be stored under refrigeration for 1 - 2 months.
Δ This breading requires very fine bread crumbs. If
'Japanese style', i.e. coarse crumbs, are available, process
for 1 or 2 minutes in a food processor to reduce the size
of the crumb.

USES
Useful breading for shrimp, chicken, steaks and chops;
for either baking or frying.

DRIED CHERRY GLAZE

YIELD   1 1/2 CUPS

INGREDIENTS

1 Cup	Water
1 tsp	Wyler's Beef Bouillon
1/2 Cup	Dried Tart Cherries
1 Tbl	Honey
1 Tbl	Brown Sugar
1 Tbl	Dry Sherry Wine ◊

Thickening
1 Tbl	Corn Starch
2 Tbls	Water

PREPARATION

In a sauce pan, mix water and bouillon. Add honey, brown sugar and sherry and bring to a boil. Make thickening in a separate container by adding corn starch and rapidly stirring in cold water, mixing completely. Δ Then slowly add to boiling mixture and stir till the glaze thickens. Remove from heat and stir in dried cherries.

HINTS

Δ To improve mixing, add cold water to the corn starch, rather than corn starch to the water.
This glaze may be stored for up to 30 days under refrigeration.

VARIATIONS

◊ Sherry may be replaced with flavored brandy.

USES

Use with poultry, veal, ham and other pork entrees.

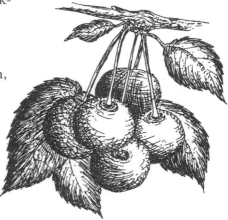

GREEK DRESSING ♣

Cooks Notes

YIELD   3 CUPS

INGREDIENTS

2 Cups	Canola Oil
3/4 Cup	Cider Vinegar
1/2 Tbl	Sugar
1/2 Tbl	Salt
1/4 tsp	Basil - fresh, chopped
1/8 tsp	White Pepper - ground
1/2 Tbl	Oregano - fresh, chopped
3/4 Tbl	Garlic Puree

PREPARATION
Mix all ingredients together well.

HINTS
May be stored, sealed, under refrigeration for up to one month.
It is always best to make dressings at least a day ahead of use, to allow the flavors to marry.

USES
In addition to use as a lettuce or pasta salad dressing, this makes a great meat and poultry marinade.

FRENCH DRESSING ♣

YIELD   5 CUPS

INGREDIENTS

1 ¹/₂ Cup	Sugar
15 oz Can	Condensed Tomato Soup
1 ¹/₈ Cup	Cider Vinegar
3 ¹/₂ tsp	Salt
3 ¹/₂ tsp	Black Pepper - ground
3 ¹/₂ tsp	Prepared Mustard
3 ¹/₂ tsp	Worcestershire Sauce
¹/₂ tsp	Garlic Puree
1 ¹/₄ Cups	Canola Oil
¹/₄	Onion

PREPARATION

In a mixing bowl, mix all ingredients, except the oil and
onion, together well. Then add oil slowly while whipping, until dressing is well blended. Take one quartered
peeled onion, separate the layers of the onion and add
onion sections to dressing.

HINTS

May be stored, sealed, under refrigeration for up to one
month.
It is always best to make dressings at least a day ahead of
use, to allow the flavors to marry.

USES

In addition to its primary use as a salad dressing, this
also makes an excellent vegetable marinade.

WHITE CREAM SAUCE

Cooks Notes

YIELD   2 CUPS

INGREDIENTS

2 Tbls	Butter
3 Tbls	Flour
2 Cups	Milk

PREPARATION
In a sauce pan, melt butter. Add flour, stirring continuously. Cook for about 5 minutes, nearly boiling the roux, carefully stirring to prevent scorching. At the same time bring milk to a scald. Mix the hot milk and the roux together, stirring vigorously. ◊

HINTS
May be stored, sealed, under refrigeration for up to seven days, if milk used in sauce has an expiration date at least that far in the future.
◊ Have milk and roux very hot prior to mixing. This will bring the sauce to a smooth, medium thick consistency quickly, with less stirring.

VARIATIONS
Wine, flavored brandy or liqueur, or herbs such as fresh basil, fresh dill or fresh rosemary may be added to create a variety of flavored cream sauces.

USES
This sauce is a basic component of some stuffings and cream sauced dishes.

PECAN BUTTER SAUCE ♣

YIELD	1 CUP

INGREDIENTS

1/4 Lb	Butter - softened
3/4 Cup	Pecans - chopped
3/4 Tbl	Lemon Juice
1 tsp	Tabasco Sauce ◊
1/2 tsp	Garlic Puree

PREPARATION

Soften butter by allowing to sit at room temperature for at least 2 hours. In a mixing bowl, combine butter, pecan pieces, lemon juice, Tabasco sauce, garlic puree, mixing all ingredients together by hand. With your hands, form the mixture into a cylindrical log about one inch in diameter, roll up in parchment paper, twist the ends of the paper tight and store in the refrigerator Δ.

HINTS

May be stored under refrigeration for up to one month. Δ For longer term storage, rather than rolling the sauce in a piece of parchment paper, divide evenly into an ice cube tray, seal, and freeze; may be stored frozen for up to six months.

VARIATIONS

◊ Vary the amount of Tabasco sauce used to change the intensity of flavor. Without the Tabasco sauce the pecan butter is a milder, yet flavorful, topping useful for many fish and chicken entrees.

USES

Cut into 1/4 inch thick portions and place on top of blackened entrees (meat, fish, or poultry) after cooking, just before serving.

CAJUN SPICE

Cooks Notes

YIELD   2 CUPS

INGREDIENTS

$^1/_2$ Cup	Paprika
$^1/_3$ Cup	White Pepper - ground
$^1/_3$ Cup	Black Pepper - coarse ground
$^1/_3$ Cup	Cayenne Pepper
$^1/_3$ Cup	Thyme - fresh, chopped
$^1/_4$ Cup	Oregano - fresh, chopped
2 Tbls	Basil - fresh, chopped

PREPARATION
Carefully mix ingredients together Δ.

HINTS
Store sealed under refrigeration, virtually forever.
Δ Be careful not to breathe deeply while mixing. This is
a very potent spice mixture.

USES
Used to blacken nearly anything - fish, seafood, poultry,
meat. Traditional blackening is a searing on high heat,
usually in an iron skillet. This mixture may be used to
'blacken' baked dishes by sprinkling on top prior to
baking.

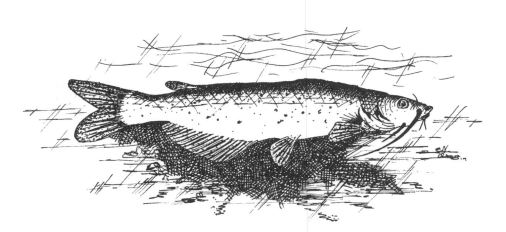

GFS®
gordon food service
Marketplace
LOCATIONS

Marquette

Sault Ste. Marie

Gaylord
Alpena

Traverse City

Cadillac

Mt. Pleasant
Midland   Bay City
Saginaw
Flint (2)

Muskegon
Grand Rapids (4)

Port Huron

Lansing (2)

Detroit (13)

Holland
Jackson   Brighton
Kalamazoo (2)
Battle Creek   Ann Arbor

Benton Harbor

Monroe

Palatine
Villa Park
Aurora   C-side
Burbank
Orland Park
Lansing
Joliet
Olympia Fields

Niles

Michigan City   Elkhart
Merrillville

Toledo (2)   Sandusky

Findlay

Fort Wayne (2)

Marion

Lafayette

Columbus (2)
Dublin
Hilliard
Trotwood
Miamisburg

Anderson

Indianapolis (3)

CANADA

GFS MARKETPLACE STORES

MICHIGAN

Alpena, MI, 49707
2400 US 23 South
(517) 358-9500

Ann Arbor, MI
3800 Carpenter Road
Ypsilanti, MI 48197
(734) 667-2500

Battle Creek, MI 49015
100 E Columbia
(616) 964-7042

Bay City, MI 48706
3730 Wilder Road
(517) 684-8601

Benton Harbor, MI 49022
1350 Mall Drive
(616) 926-2000

Brighton, MI 48116
8144 W Grand River Avenue
(810 220-0110

Cadillac, MI 49601
1578 N Mitchell
(231) 779-4300

Chesterfield Township, MI 48047
51630 Gratiot Avenue
(810) 948-2839

Dearborn, MI 48127
5720 N Telegraph Road
(313) 792-9367

Farmington Hills, MI 48335
39047 Grand River Avenue
(248) 474-1990

Flint-Burton, MI
1507 Walli-Strasse
Burton, MI 48509
(810) 743-0223

Flint, MI 48532
2195 S Linden Road
(810) 732-4242

Gaylord, MI 49735
1466 M-32 West
(517) 731-0404

Grand Rapids, MI
2929 29th Street SE
Kentwood, MI 49512
(616) 956-9545

Grand Rapids, MI 49321
4322 Alpine Avenue
(616) 785-8780

Grand Rapids, MI 49548
4990 Clay Avenue
(616) 538-4812

Holland, MI 49424
12600 Felch
(616) 786-3300

Jackson, MI 49202
1507 Boardman Road
(517) 783-1855

Jenison, MI 49428
7434 Cottonwood Drive
(616) 667-0211

Kalamazoo, MI 49009
827 N Drake Road
(616) 373-3000

Kalamazoo, MI 49001
1801 Sprinkle Road
(616) 381-1020

Lansing, MI 48911
454 E Edgewood
(517) 887-0750

Lansing, MI 48917
5912 West Saginaw
(517) 886-5565

Marquette, MI 49855
3480 US 41 West
(906) 226-9063

Midland, MI 48640
1511 Joe Mann Blvd
(517) 837-3098

Monroe, MI 48162
1733 Telegraph Road
(734) 243-3500

Mount Clemens, MI
35400 Groesbeck
Clinton Township, MI 48035
(810) 792-7600

Mount Pleasant, MI 48858
1706 S Mission Street
(517) 772-8776

Muskegon, MI 49444
525 W Sherman Blvd
(231) 733-0374

Niles, MI 49120
2911 S 11th Street
(616) 684-7720

Pontiac, MI
4295 Highland Road
Waterford, MI 48328
(248) 738-7736

Port Huron, MI
4605 24th Avenue
Fort Gratiot, MI 48059
(810) 385-4400

Rochester Hills, MI 48309
1370 Walton Blvd
(248) 656-6000

Sault St. Marie, MI 49783
31951 I-75 Business Spur
(906) 635-6100

Saginaw, MI 48603
3800 Bay Road
(517) 792-2433

Southfield, MI 48034
24475 Telegraph Road
(248) 827-8584

Taylor, MI 48180
10065 Telegraph Road
(313) 291-0360

Traverse City, MI 49684
2487 Rice Street
(231) 922-4999

Troy, MI 48083
2822 E Maple
(248) 588-1700

Utica, MI 48315
45331 Utica Park Blvd
(810) 254-5656

Warren, MI 48092
7835 Convention Road
(810) 983-5405

Westland, MI 48185
38150 Ford Road
(734) 721-8700

Wixom, MI 48393
49200 Wixon Tech Drive
(248) 926-0353

INDIANA

Anderson, IN 46013
2110 East 53rd Street
(765) 642-6254

Elkhart, IN 46514
2700 Cassopolis
(219) 264-5913

Ft. Wayne, IN 46825
4621 Speedway Drive
(219) 484-2548

Ft. Wayne, IN 46804
5507 Illinois Road
(219) 436-6109

Indianapolis-Greenwood, IN
790 North US 31
Greenwood, IN 46142
(317) 882-0700

Indianapolis-Lafayette, IN 46254
4574 Lafayette Road
(317) 388-0101

Indianapolis-Shadeland, IN 46226
3110 N Shadeland Avenue
(317) 549-2000

Lafayette, IN 47905
115 N Farabee Drive
(765) 447-4767

Merrillville, IN 46410
1601 West 81st Avenue
(219) 756-4200

Michigan City, IN 46360
5400 Franklin
(219) 874-6295

ILLINOIS

Auroa, IL 60504
4101 Healthway
(630) 375-9017

Burbank, IL 60459
8146 S Cicero
(708) 424-4335

Countryside, IL 60525
9930 Joliet Road
(708) 354-1053

Joliet, IL 60435
2901 West Jefferson
(815) 729-2859

Lansing, IL 60438
2330 173rd Street
(708) 474-7163

Olympia Fields, IL 60461
20930 S Crawford Avenue
(708) 747-7072

Orland Park, IL 60462
15606 Harlem Avenue
(708) 532-0794

Palatine, IL 60074
1930 N Rand Road
(847) 934-0403

Villa Park, IL 60181
220 E Roosevelt Road
(630) 832-3354

OHIO

Colombus-Hilliard 43228
1935 Hilliard Rome Road
Columbus, OH 43228
(614) 529-8846

Columbus-Minerva 43228
5400 Cleveland Avenue
(614) 891-8686

Columbus-Tussing 43068
6375 Tussing Road
(614) 861-0916

Dublin, OH 43017
3901 Dublin/Grandville Road
(614) 766-5551

Findlay, OH 45840
2301 Tiffin Avenue
(419) 423-9503

Marion, OH 43302
1672 Marion Mt. Gilead Road
(740) 386-5128

Miamisburg, OH 45342
8499 B Springboro Pike SR 741
(937) 435-6905

Sandusky, OH 44870
3818 Milan Road
(419) 621-0799

Toledo, OH 43612
609 West Alexis Road
(419) 478-5444

Toledo, OH
1450 Holland Road
Maumee,OH 43537
(419) 893-5035

Trotwood, OH 45426
5380 Salem
(937) 854-7480

INDEX

Additional copies of this book are available
for $21.95 plus $3.50 for postage and handling.
(Canadian Orders CDN plus $4.00)

By mail:
The Leelanau Country Inn
149 East Harbor Highway
Maple City, MI 49664

Or, by telephone from 9 am to 5 pm:
800 - COOK 441

VISA - MasterCard

Volume purchase discounts available.

For Trade Orders Please Contact:

Partners Book Distributing
2325 Jarco Dr.
Holt, MI 48842

Voice: 800-336-3137
Fax: 517-694-0617